ESSENTIALS OF THE UNIFICATION PRINCIPLE

ESSENTIALS OF THE UNIFICATION PRINCIPLE

The Core Teachings of
Sun Myung Moon

The Interreligious Leadership Seminar
481 8th Avenue
New York, New York 10001

ISBN 0-910621-70-5

Cover Design by Jonathan Gullery

Printed in the United States of America

TABLE OF
CONTENTS

TABLE OF
CONTENTS
IN CHAPTER SECTIONS

PREFACE

As the world prepares for the 21st Century it is confronted with a host of challenges: inter-religious and ethnic conflicts; increasing threats to man's environment; growing drug abuse, corruption, crime and terrorism; deepening moral decline and the scourge of AIDS. And yet this is an age of unprecedented development in science and technology, development which gives modern men and women awesome power to shape their lives and destiny. There is a paradox here: human beings are daily increasing their knowledge of the world and yet seem less and less able to solve the fundamental problems of life.

Religion claims to have the solution to this human dilemma, but in today's science-dominated world many people are cynical about religion, pointing to the many failures and hypocrisies in its practice over the centuries. Understandably, they question belief systems that claim to solve human problems and save people from evil but have not succeeded in ending human conflict and suffering.

Despite inadequacies in the practice of religion to date, however, human beings cannot expect to meet the challenges of life without understanding their Creator and His purpose for the universe. The world of result cannot be understood without knowledge of the world of cause. One should ask, then: amidst the crisis and confusion of the 20th Century world, where is God to be found? What is He thinking and doing today and what are His solutions for the problems facing humanity? The Unification Principle addresses these and other critical questions, providing a modern-day understanding of God and His desire for humankind.

The Principle is the essential teaching of Sun Myung Moon, a Korean man of God who from early youth has passionately searched for lasting solutions to the fundamental problems of life and devoted himself completely to the service of God and humanity. He has been scorned by most of the world but has persevered in his responsibility, patiently explaining the need for a new understanding of God and radical solutions for age-old and contemporary problems.

This summary of the Principle has been prepared with two modernday concerns in mind: 1. the need for inter-religious understanding and harmony, and 2. the need for an understanding of God and the creation that is fully compatible with science. Without quoting directly from the sacred books, it sets out an understanding of God and human beings that sheds light on existing scriptures and offers a spiritual framework for life.

The value of the Principle is demonstrated in the fruitful lives of hundreds of thousands of people around the world who are guided by its insights. Furthermore, the Principle provides the inspirational foundation for dozens of projects to benefit humankind, from inter-religious, cultural and scientific initiatives to relief programs, educational institutions and quality publications.

I invite you to study it carefully and prayerfully to see why so many people from all walks of life and every corner of the earth have made the Unification Principle the basis for their lives of faith and, through its application, have created happy and healthy families within a global community of enlightened believers. I myself have followed the path of the Principle for almost four decades and can assure you that your study of it will benefit your life greatly.

CHUNG HWAN KWAK
Seoul, Korea
1 May 1993

INTRODUCTION

The Unification Principle, or simply the Principle, is a religious teaching that addresses the fundamental questions of existence: where do human beings come from? How were they created and how are they to relate with nature? Is there a supreme creator, God? If so, what is God's nature and why did He create human beings? If there is a purpose to human life, how can it be fulfilled? Why is there evil and where did it come from? If God is good, what has He been doing to end human suffering and what is His will for humankind today?

The Principle was discovered by the founder and leader of the Unification Movement, Sun Myung Moon. As he grew up in his native Korea, he became intensely aware of human suffering and the failure of humanity to create a loving and just world. He sought to understand why people suffer and how suffering can be ended. Raised in a Christian family, he knew that religion addressed the fundamental human condition and promised an ideal world to those who obey God. But he saw that established religions, although centuries old and based on scriptures offering revelatory insights, were, in practice, unable to answer many of life's questions or solve the deepest problems facing humankind. Furthermore, due to the inadequacy of their understanding of scriptures, religious scholars and leaders were not succeeding in a fundamental task of religion: preparation of humanity for the advent of a messianic figure who would establish an ideal world under God. Troubled by the immense gap between religious ideals and the actual state of the world, he began his own ardent pursuit of solutions through a life of prayer and study.

At age sixteen, while deep in prayer on a mountainside near his village, he had a vision of Jesus Christ, who called him to dedicate his life to God and the salvation of humankind. Despite his youth and the seeming impossibility of ending human suffering and injustice, he accepted God's call and embarked on a life of complete obedience to the will of God. Because of his unwavering commitment to this mission, he has faced great hardship and persecution, but he has never deviated from his chosen path.

After receiving his commission from God, he knew he could not succeed in his task without a profound understanding of the Creator and His creation. He intensified his quest for the truth, spending days and nights in passionate prayer, in rigorous fasting and study. His method was to posit specific questions about God, Satan and humanity, research answers in the physical and spiritual worlds, and then seek confirmation for those answers through prayer. On several occasions he was guided directly by Abraham, Moses, Jesus, Mohammed, Buddha and other saints and sages of all faiths, who met him in spirit and contributed to his understanding of God and the complex history of God's relationship with humankind. By the age of 25 he had developed the fundamentals of the Unification Principle, the understanding introduced in this book.

The Principle provides insights into the nature of God and humanity, the reason men and women were created and the way human society can be ordered to please God *and* satisfy the inherent aspirations of men and women. It also explains how human beings should relate to their environment. Furthermore, it examines how and why the first human ancestors separated from God, how this separation can be ended and what God has been doing in history to restore human beings to a state of oneness with their Creator.

The Principle is the basis for the Unification Movement, which is not a legal entity but the activities, projects and organizations inspired by the vision and teaching of Sun Myung Moon. Most of these initiatives, which range from inter-religious and international cultural foundations to universities and global news organizations, were founded by him and all of them are guided by the ideals and understanding contained in the Principle. There are several organizations throughout the world that group together individuals who study the Principle and seek to apply its insights and instructions to their lives. The Principle promotes mutual understanding and harmony among people of all faiths and offers a religious vision that can benefit anyone seeking truth. Thus, although religious in inspiration, the Unification Movement is not a new religion and does not seek to compete with existing religions.

This book was prepared primarily for members of the monotheistic faiths, including readers from Judeo-Christian and Muslim cultures who were raised in secular homes and never given a formal religious education but are generally familiar with the main figures and historical events of religious tradition. Much of the content is related to Biblical and Koranic scriptures, although without direct quotation. (Other explanations of the Principle, either in print already or under development, relate it directly to major world scriptures. A philosophical explanation of the Principle, called Unification Thought, presents theories of the original image, ontology, the original human nature, epistemology, logic, axiology, ethics, education, art, history and methodology.)

Scriptural references have been omitted from this text for two reasons. First, many people today lack a specific knowledge of scriptures altogether, even though they might come from nominally religious homes. For them, the scriptural base for a teaching is irrelevant. Second, all too often scriptures are used as ammunition in the theological disputes that divide religions into sects and separate one religion from another. This text is intended to promote understanding among believers of all faiths and does not use scriptures to support its position.

Readers are encouraged to study the Principle as an integrated teaching, a logical sequence of ideas and insights that, taken in its parts and as a whole, sheds new light on life and history, as well as illuminating existing scriptures. Those well versed in a particular holy book will recognize corroborating links between scriptural passages familiar to them and elements of the Principle. In general, this explanation of the Principle stands on religious history as agreed by most Jews, Christians and Muslims, with major differences acknowledged. The interpretation of history is unique to the Principle.

The basis for adding a new interpretation of scriptures for the enlightenment of those who seek a deeper knowledge of God and creation exists in the scriptures themselves. The Christian Bible contains the words and deeds of Jesus and his early followers, as the New Testament, as well as the Torah and other Jewish sacred texts, included as the Old Testament. In this way Christians accept the Jewish scriptures as their own, but interpret them according to their own beliefs, which are derived primarily from the New Testament. In the Koran God says, "We sent the scripture in truth, confirming the scripture that came before it, and guarding it." (S5, 48) Some Muslim scholars (Yusuf Ali, e.g.) refer extensively to the Bible in their commentaries on the Koran, especially in filling out the sacred history presented in the Koran. Muslims interpret both Jewish and Christian scriptures according to the Koran. Both Christians and Muslims recognize that God revealed truth through the earlier scriptures.

Many concepts from the other great faiths (Hinduism, Buddhism, Taoism, Confucianism and Zoroastrianism) are found within the Principle and the basic beliefs and histories of these global religions are briefly outlined in Chapter 16.

The Principle covers three major topics: the ideal of God's creation, the failure of humans to fulfill that ideal and the divinely-guided process of human development, through history, towards the restoration of God's ideal.

The first part, The Principles of Creation, discusses the nature of God, human beings and the rest of creation, as well as God's purpose in making all beings and the way that purpose can be realized. It examines what the world would be like if sin was absent from human affairs and everyone obeyed God. This ideal world embodies the highest dreams and aspirations of all people: a fruitful, peaceful and joyful existence. The first part also explains the process of spiritual growth and the nature of the spirit world, humanity's eternal home.

The second part, The Human Fall, explains the destiny of the original human beings and explores the reasons for human suffering and the extreme aberrations of human behavior evident everywhere in contradiction to the ideal of people living happy lives of family love. It discusses the results of the fall in human nature, history and the modern world, delineating the remedies that are needed. Without knowing the root cause of humanity's separation from God it is impossible for humans to understand their history of sin and suffering and the contemporary godless state of the world.

The third part, The History of Restoration, explains God's work to restore original, pure love to fallen men and women, and the response of humankind to God over the ages. This explanation relates the main figures and events of sacred history to the principles of restoration, which are the principles of creation as they operate to restore fallen people. The lives of Adam, Noah, Abraham, Moses, Jesus and Mohammed are among those examined within the framework of the plan for providential history.

This book was prepared with the approval of Chung Hwan Kwak, author of *Outline of the Principle, Level 4*, a standard text. It's contents are drawn from hundreds of speeches made by Sun Myung Moon and are organized along the lines of *Level 4*. It was written primarily by Thomas Cromwell, who has been the Unification Movement representative in the Middle East for the past 18 years, and includes extensive input from Frank Kaufmann (who contributed all of Chapter 16), Andrew Wilson, Tyler Hendricks, Taj Hamad, Csilla Balint and Jennifer Symon, all of whom hold relevant academic degrees and are experienced lecturers on the Principle. Any errors or misrepresentations in the text are entirely the fault of the author, and any questions or comments about the text can be sent to him at the address below.

THOMAS CROMWELL
P.O.Box 30182
10033 Athens
Greece

PART

I

THE PRINCIPLES OF CREATION

1 | GOD AND CREATION

INTRODUCTION

The fundamental questions about life and the universe cannot be answered conclusively without understanding the nature of God, the Creator. The cosmos did not create itself but was created by invisible God, the Prime Cause of all resultant beings. To understand the result, one must know the cause and how it relates to the effect; to understand the existence of human beings and their environment one must understand God and the principles by which all things were created.

Although the vast majority of human beings believe in God, or some type of transcendent spiritual force or principle, the invisibility of God makes it difficult for earth-bound humans to understand Him, His nature, His purpose in creating humankind and His desire for humanity in the contemporary world.

The Unification Principle is an explanation of humanity and nature based on belief in the existence of God, the good Creator of all beings and the origin of the principles that govern human life, spiritual and physical. The Principle demonstrates God's existence as revealed in His creation and in the history of humankind and explains the relationship between Creator and creation.

To understand any creator one must study the fruits of his creative labors and the biography of his life to see what his works and actions reveal about his nature. For example, in order to understand the character of an author whom you cannot meet face to face, you would study his literary output and life history to discover what they tell you about his personality. Thus for humans to un-

derstand God, they must study God's creation, especially humankind, the crowning perfection of God's creative work; and
they must examine the record of God's activities through the ages,
especially as written in the sacred histories of humanity.

The Resemblance Between God and Creation

The creation is rich in its diversity and yet all the various parts
hold together in an intricate matrix of relationships. For such integrity to prevail, there must be common elements among existing
beings, organic and inorganic, which make this unity possible.
Close examination of the creation reveals that the evident differences between fire and water, ants and elephants, human beings
and rocks disguise the fact that all beings are part of a universal
resemblance and harmonious order. It is reasonable to assume that
the universal characteristics of creation derive from attributes of a
common creator.

The Dual Characteristics of Creation

The elements common to all creation are called *dual characteristics*. Every being has dual characteristics derived from the dual attributes of the Creator, God. There are two basic types of dual
characteristics. The most fundamental is *internal character* and *external form*. The internal character gives a being purpose and direction, while the external form embodies and expresses that character in a tangible structure, and completes the unique identity of
a being. The secondary type of duality, *positivity* and *negativity*,
enables every being to interact with others. Positivity and negativity are not value-related, but complementary characteristics that
make it possible for two or more entities to relate with one another and create a harmonious union in which each partner is completed through its relationship with the other.

   The two types of dual characteristics are clearly evident in human beings. Both men and women are endowed with internal
character (mind) and external form (body) which together create

the human identity with its unique internal and external attributes. However, while men and women share certain characteristics as human beings, they also have internal and external differences which distinguish the sexes from each other. It is because men and women have so much in common as humans, but are also differentiated into two distinct yet complementary groups, that when a man and a woman unite in pure love they experience complete fulfillment. Out of that union new life is produced and creation is multiplied. Thus both types of dual characteristics are essential for the completion and continuation of creation.

The creation is ordered hierarchically, with human beings at the center, supported by animals and then plants, and with all organic creatures sustained by the mineral kingdom. This hierarchy of creation is itself sustained by a second hierarchy, the molecules, atoms and sub-atomic particles of which every creation is made. The great beauty of nature is produced by the harmonization of dual characteristics within and among all the hierarchies of created beings.

Internal Character and External Form

Every being in these natural hierarchies has internal character and external form. The internal character of a human being is mind, which guides the external form, or body, imbuing it with purpose and direction. Action flows from thought such that the patterns of an individual's thinking are written in his body language and behavior. For this reason, one can learn about a person's invisible mind by studying its external manifestations in his body. A loving, generous person will radiate goodness and kindness in appearance and activity, whereas a selfish and greedy person will have an unattractive personality and always take from others.

Animal character and behavior is shaped by instinctive mind. Without instruction, birds make nests in which to lay eggs and nurture their young, salmon return to their freshwater spawning grounds to procreate after years at sea, beavers construct dams to create environments that support their families and ants organize themselves into armies to build homes and procure food. Every type of animal has its own, special internal character embodied in a unique external form. Through its body, an animal's fear, anger or affection are communicated, as when a dog cringes, barks or wags its tail. The wondrous variety and unity of the animal kingdom demonstrates the creative diversity within the oneness of God.

Plants can be said to have mind-like elements, or inherent directive natures, that determine their structures and natural functions and respond to environmental influences. Plants can grow towards sunlight, up the sides of buildings or away from dangerous elements. Experiments have shown that they respond to human affection and gentle music. All of these behavioral traits of plants are functions of their invisible internal characters. The earth's flora is made up of millions of plant varieties. Each plays a particular part within the whole, and is harmonized with the rest of creation within God's overall purpose for nature.

Molecules, and the chemical compounds they form, possess unique qualities and demonstrate specific behavior. For example, water, which is the combination of two hydrogen atoms with one oxygen atom, has properties that allow it to combine with a wide variety of different molecules to create a vast range of substances. However, these same properties also prevent it from combining with certain other molecules. This behavior of water is governed by its invisible internal characteristics, manifest in its molecular structure. Water, like all molecules, was created by God to fulfill a specific purpose within the overall design for creation.

Atoms are organized into nine groups within the periodic table of elements. Each group demonstrates certain behavioral characteristics, ranging from great combinability (the carbon family) to total non-combinability (the inert elements). The invisible internal character of atoms, expressed in their atomic structures, determines their behavior.

Atoms are composed of sub-atomic particles, primarily neutrons and positively-charged protons in the nucleus and negatively-charged electrons surrounding the nucleus. There are several other particles as well. Sub-atomic particles combine to form the different atoms with their diverse characteristics. For example, the nucleus of a hydrogen atom has one neutron and one proton, circled by one electron. The nature of hydrogen is to give away its electron in the formation of molecules, making it an ion with a positive charge of one. Oxygen has eight protons and eight electrons and the nature to receive two electrons in the formation of molecules, making it an ion with a negative charge of two. The two negative charges of the oxygen ion enable it to combine with two positively-charged hydrogen ions to form water, a very stable molecule.

Science recognizes the internal character of the creation without defining it as such. Scientists speak of the "behavior" of molecules, atoms and particles, implying the existence of their inner nature without specifying what it is. And science has shown that the border between tangible matter and invisible energy exists only in human minds and not in creation itself. This means that inorganic creations, as well as organic ones, are just the external forms of invisible essence. It is at the center of this invisible, energic dimension of creation that the causal world of spirit and mind exists.

Harmony of the Creation

The purposefulness and order so evident in the creation derive from the unity of its invisible internal character and are expressions of the volition and unity of its invisible Creator, God. God made every being with an individual purpose that contributes to the purpose of the whole such that individual purpose is realized through the realization of the purpose of the whole. The diversity and beauty of the creation reflect the manifold beauty of God's nature, while its integrity and harmony result from His oneness and His single, unifying purpose for the whole creation.

Positivity and Negativity

While internal character and external form are the primary dual characteristics in shaping the identity of beings, there are secondary dual characteristics, positivity and negativity, that differentiate creations into complementary pairs. Human beings and animals are either males or females, while flowers have their own forms of masculinity and femininity (stamen and pistil). The molecules, atoms and particles also exist as positive or negative opposites: cations and anions, protons and electrons. Where the positive-negative differentiation is not apparent in two separate entities, it exists within individual beings, as demonstrated, for example, when a cell's nucleus and cytoplasm divide in asexual reproduction.

The dual characteristics of positivity and negativity are also clearly evident in the structures of created beings. For example, the human body functions through the interaction of many paired parts, such as the two eyes, ears, nostrils, lips, arms, legs, lungs, kidneys, etc. Human beings exist and act physically through the cooperation between the dual characteristics of their bodies. The same principle applies to all the creation.

The Dual Characteristics of God

The dual characteristics of creation are derived from the dual attributes of God. The Internal Character of God is *Heart*, the origin of emotion, intellect and will, and God's External Form is *Universal Prime Energy*. God's positivity and negativity are prime masculinity and prime femininity.

Within God, there are no divisions between attributes. The dual characteristics of God's being are perfectly harmonized in the complete unity of divine oneness. Therefore, God's dual characteristics can only be recognized as they are manifested in the creation or as they are evidenced to humanity through revelation.

God's most internal and fundamental nature is heart, the irrepressible impulse to experience joy through love. God's Heart is the foundation of His being and oneness, the source of His love and the origin of His purpose in making the creation. God's love is expressed in the manifestations of the Universal Prime Energy, out of which the creation was made. The essence of heart is the parental desire to create and love offspring. Hence God's creation of human beings must above all be understood as an act of parental love. (The parent–child relationship between God and humans is a kinship of love not to be confused with a biological relationship.)

In this text, God is referred to as "Him" for simplicity's sake, even though God created both men and women and therefore must have both masculinity and femininity within a unified nature. In the relationship between God and human beings, God, as Creator, takes an initiating, masculine role to the responsive, feminine role of the humans He created.

The Principles of Creation

God created everything according to principles which derive from the principles of His own perfect being. By these principles all things came into existence, and through them creation is governed by its Creator. The relations within and among all created beings are guided towards harmonization and mutual fulfillment by the same principles. It is these principles which religions seek to articulate in spiritual laws of faith and conduct and which science tries to define in physical laws of the universe. Because there is only one God, His principles are universal and are the basis for the common truths found in all valid religions and sciences. They are called the *principles of creation*.

By understanding the principles of creation humans can comprehend the laws that lie behind God's commandments and can learn to live in full accordance with God's will. They can also reconcile the inner world of religion with the external world of science.

Conclusion

The creation resembles its Creator, God, in the duality of its structure, internal and external, positive and negative. As the Creator, God is the source of the unifying purpose and principles that govern the creation and its relationship with God. The nature of the interaction between God and the creation, as well as that among the various created beings, will be examined in the next chapter.

2 | THE STRUCTURE AND FUNCTION OF THE CREATION

INTRODUCTION

The universe is not a random grouping of disassociated entities moving aimlessly through time and space, but rather a finely-balanced system of interrelated beings which interact in an orderly fashion, guided by a unifying purpose. If this were not so, there would be no basis for science, which presupposes the existence of common elements and universal laws in the cosmos and works to identify and understand them. But science cannot provide a complete picture of reality without a complementary understanding of the internal dimensions of the creation. As shown in the previous chapter, the order and harmony of the universe result from the character and purpose with which God endowed the invisible, internal elements of creation. It is the external manifestations of these internal realities that are known to science.

Because science is limited to examination of the external world, it leaves a number of important questions unanswered, such as: How does God maintain a relationship with the creation? How does the invisible world of cause interface with the visible world of creation? What is the origin and basis for existence and life? What are the universal dynamics of relationships between dual characteristics? What are the fundamental structures of creation that enable it to exist and develop? These are some of the questions addressed in this chapter.

Subjects and Objects

The dual characteristics of any creation exist in dynamic relationship with each other. In order for there to be interaction between them, one must initiate the relationship and the other respond. The Principle calls the initiator a *subject* and the responding partner an *object*. God is the Prime Subject, the creation His object. Within the creation, humans are subject to all other beings, which, in turn, are ordered into hierarchies of subject-object relations. Through this chain of being, all creations are connected to the Creator, God, the source of existence and life, and the various individual creations are tied into a harmonious whole. As Subject of the whole cosmos, God is the Internal Character to creation's external form, the masculine initiator to creation's responsive, feminine nature.

The hierarchies of subject-object relationships link the various species, kinds and kingdoms of creation to God. At the same time, the myriad subject-object interactions maintain and develop each subdivision of nature. For example, protons and electrons interact to form atoms; cations and anions combine to form molecules; plants multiply through cross-pollination between stamens and pistils; and animals multiply through mating between males and females.

Every creation exists through the maintenance of subject-object relations between its component parts. Thus, a human being maintains life through millions of subject-object relationships: between cells, organs, limbs, nerve and circulatory systems, and so on. The heart and lungs interact to bring oxygen into the bloodstream, while the arteries and veins circulate the blood throughout the body. The central and peripheral nervous systems coordinate the functions of the body, including the interaction of muscle and skeleton. In this example, nerves, directed by the brain, are subject and the muscles they control are their object. However, the muscles in turn are the subject of the bones. Every part of the human body fulfills its purpose through its subject-object relations with other parts.

Universal Prime Force

How does God relate to the countless subjects and objects He has created? In order for energy to act it must have a conduit for its action, and in order for God to interact with the creation there must be a base in creation to receive God's energy. The subject-object pairs in the creation provide circuits through which God's love and power can flow. Subjects and objects are created in the image of God's being, which has its own subject and object attributes. By reflecting God's nature they share common elements with God, making possible the flow of energy between God and His creation. When Universal Prime Energy, the External Form of God, acts, it becomes *universal prime force*. God endows His creation with universal prime force, which is the directed energy that sustains creation's existence, action and multiplication. The universal prime force links God to His creation and empowers its dynamism.

Giving and Receiving Action

Through the action of universal prime force, each subject is brought into a relationship with a given object to complete itself. Subjects and objects separated from each other in the creation are partial reflections of the unity of God, whereas joined in harmony they reflect, at their proper level, the complete unity of subject and object within God.

Subject and object need a common base, that is mutuality of characteristics, in order to interact. When they do establish a common base, through the action of universal prime force in both of them, they create a relationship of giving and receiving energy from each other. This *giving and receiving action* draws the subject and object together until each finds completion through its relationship with the other, creating a unity that resembles the subject-object unity of the attributes of their Creator, God.

When subjects and objects are empowered by universal prime force to create harmonious relationships, they engage in giving and receiving action and generate *forces of giving and receiving action.* These are the substantial foundation for life itself: existence, action and multiplication. Universal Prime Energy is the intangible source of life and the universal prime force is the intangible foundation for life. The forces of giving and receiving action are the tangible, substantial foundation for life.

Existence and life are possible only when there is a flow of energy between subject and object, with both of them giving and receiving. Breathing would not work if humans only inhaled; circulation would not work if humans only had arteries to take blood from the heart to the body but lacked veins to return it to the heart. Thus all creation is maintained and develops through the giving and receiving between subjects and objects.

Many of the subject-object pairs and the forces of giving and receiving action that they generate have been identified by science. For example, nuclear power, electricity, heat and light are energies produced by interaction between atoms or sub-atomic particles; gravitational energy is produced by the interaction between heavenly bodies, and so on. The foundations for the natural world are created when protons and electrons, empowered by universal prime force, give and receive energy to form atoms which, as cations and anions, give and receive atomic forces in the creation of molecules.

The reproductive dimension of life is evident in the plant, animal and human kingdoms. (Because only human beings were created with eternal spiritual natures, they should be distinguished from animals.) In plants, stamens and pistils interact to produce the biological forces necessary for the creation of seeds. Male and female animals mate to produce offspring. Men and women are made by God as subjects and objects who are endowed with complementary characteristics, both internal and external, which enable them to form harmonious and productive couples. Man's spiritual and physical masculinity is balanced perfectly by woman's spiritual and physical femininity.

It is a man's nature to seek completion through becoming one with a woman, while the woman's feminine nature seeks completion through union with a masculine subject. In perfect unity the two become as one, resembling the oneness of God. Since man and woman are the culmination of God's creation and the encapsulation of the physical and spiritual realms, when they unite they become the completed image of God, the full embodiment of His attributes.

The forces of giving and receiving action produced by their union are the foundation for their lives and for the creation of their family.

Individual Truth Bodies

God's oneness is manifested in the perfect union between His subject and object attributes: divine Internal Character and External Form, Positivity and Negativity. Each creation is endowed with dual characteristics that are a reflection of God's dual attributes. Human beings are the most complete embodiment of God's nature and can be considered the image of God. Their spiritual natures are the most complete reflection of God's internal attributes, and their bodies the most complete reflection of His external attributes. The rest of creation was made in the image of humans and is a symbolic reflection of God's attributes.

God is Truth: the true relationship between His dual attributes. This perfection of being is maintained through totally harmonious giving and receiving relationships between His attributes within His oneness. The word of God, as revealed to humankind, is an articulation of His existential truth. Whenever a creation becomes a unified being of harmonized dual characteristics, and thus reflects the unity of God, it becomes an embodiment of Truth, or an *individual truth body*. All the creation, from atoms to human beings, was made by God to resemble His true nature and to find fulfillment through completing that resemblance.

Every created being has a part to play in creation as a whole. It completes itself as an individual truth body by fulfilling its role within the created order. When a cation is formed from the interaction of protons and electrons, and then seeks out an anion to form a molecule, it is fulfilling its God-given purpose to become an individual truth body within the universe of God's creation.

Human individual truth bodies are perfected when men and women grow to maturity by uniting mind and body and then forming harmonious families. A *true man* unites his mind and body into perfect oneness and then forms a union of love with a *true woman* to create a family, according to God's purpose for them. Together, they are the complete embodiment of the dual characteristics of God, internal and external, male and female. Unified, a true man and woman become *true parents,* qualified to give birth to *true children.* These *true sons* and *true daughters* grow up as *true brothers* and *true sisters* to become *true husbands* and *true wives,* finally becoming true parents themselves: each man perfecting his resemblance of God's masculinity, each woman perfecting her resemblance of God's femininity. Through true parents, true men and women are multiplied in God's creation.

True Love

The fundamental nature of God's Heart is to give unconditionally. This impulse is called love. As a manifestation of the true being of God, the love of God is *true love.* Universal prime force is imbued with purpose and direction by God's true love, the absolute, unconditional love of God for His creation. Since the true love of God is the source of life for human beings and the rest of creation, essentially, God is Love.

God created men and women to drink eternally at the inexhaustible fountain of His true love. A true man and true woman have the characteristics to be fully endowed with God's love so that they can become true parents, giving and receiving true love with each other, their family members and other true men and women. Their love becomes an extension of God's love. When God, a true man and a true woman come together in a unity of true love, a foundation is created for the birth and education of true children. When these children are raised by true parents in homes of true love they will become true men and women themselves. The true love that flows through a true family is the foundation for the creation of a true society, nation and world. In this way, the true love, life and lineage of God are inherited by humankind.

The Four Position Foundation

True love flows wherever there are true subject-object relationships in the image of God's own internal harmony. The model for these ideal relationships in human society is reproduced throughout the rest of creation in symbolic reflection of God's unity. Universally, when subjects and objects energized by universal prime force interact in accordance with God's will, they come to reflect God, who is the perfect union of subject and object attributes. Secondly, their interaction creates a new entity which embodies elements of both of them. This new creation adds a fourth position to the three occupied by God, the subject and the object. All four, interacting with one another, complete a *four position foundation* for the fulfillment of the purpose of existence.

The Triple Object Purpose

Through giving and receiving with one another, the four participants become as one, and each fulfills its purpose through its relations with the other three. Through developing these qualitatively different relationships with three other members of the four position foundation, each member can fulfill its potential. For example, the subject fulfills its purpose through perfecting its relationships with God, the object and the new entity created by its interaction with the object, while the object fulfills its purpose through perfecting its relationships with God, the subject and the new creation. Thus the four position foundation is completed through fulfillment of the *triple object purpose*.

The Four Position Foundation in Creation

Examples of the formation of four position foundations in creation are protons (subjects) and electrons (objects) interacting to form atoms (new creations); stamens and pistils relating to produce seeds; male and female animals mating to produce offspring and husbands and wives uniting in love to have children.

Throughout the cosmos, all beings have the nature to establish four position foundations. Since the creation is ordered hierarchically and only humans are endowed with an internal character capable of knowing God directly, within the world of nature God's position in the four position foundation is represented by man. For those creations not directly connected to people, the position of human beings as God's representatives is assumed by the hierarchy of nature, centered on humans. Through this hierarchy, God's purpose is imparted to all four position foundations in creation.

Since the natural world was created as an environment to sustain human beings, the animal, plant and mineral kingdoms exist for humankind. Each level of creation fulfills its purpose through completing four position foundations that contribute to fulfilling the purpose of the next higher level. Thus sub-atomic particles interact centered on the purpose of atoms, cations and anions on the purpose of molecules and molecules on the purpose of the created beings they form. The plants and animals in God's creation are ordered so that lower life forms support higher ones. For example, in a food chain the lower serves the higher: grass, nourished by mineral-rich soil, is eaten by insects, in turn eaten by snakes and frogs, which are then eaten by birds and small carnivores. Humans live from plants and animals that are themselves sustained by lower plant or animal species. Plants and animals all fulfill their purposes by contributing to the existence of human beings. Ultimately this allows lower beings to participate in the direct encounter with God, which is unique to man.

The Family Unit

In human society there are many examples of four position foundations but the family unit is the most important. Only through the family can individuals be fulfilled completely.

Since men and women were made by God to be the objects of His true love, their most fundamental desire is for love. This desire can only be satisfied fully in the family, because it is in the family that people can learn to receive and give true love in all its dimensions. The natural love relationships within families are all part of God's ideal. So too are extra-familial love relationships that contribute to the creation of God-centered families and a God-centered world, such as love of neighbors and friends, of society and country. All extra-familial love relationships are direct reflections of one of the various relationships that comprise familial love.

Any human relationship guided by self-centered rather than God-centered purposes, such as sexual intercourse outside a commitment to marriage and family, or possessive parental love at the cost of a child's well-being, is based on false love. True love is to sacrifice yourself for others, whereas false love is to sacrifice others for yourself. True love allows only one, eternal spouse, one man-woman union for the creation of a God-centered four position foundation. Only in such a single-spouse family can love be perfected and man's purpose be fulfilled. False love relationships violate the order of God's creation and thus destroy individuals, families, societies and nations.

Children are born needing the love of their parents. As infants, their consciousness is oriented more to receiving than giving. As children grow, they learn to give love as well as receive it — with their parents, siblings and friends. Once a boy reaches maturity and becomes a man, he is qualified to enter into a relationship of conjugal love with a similarly mature woman. On the foundation of this responsible husband-wife relationship, a couple is qualified to have children, to whom they give unconditional love.

God's love for His creation is unconditional, that is, it is given without requiring or demanding a reciprocation of love. Human love comes to resemble this true love of God when people learn to give unconditional love to others. The family is the only environment where true, unconditional love can be perfected, because only true parents are capable of giving this standard of love, and the only way to become a true parent is to establish a God-centered family.

The practice of true love creates a heavenly atmosphere among all those who participate in it. In an environment of true love, all human problems and misery can be eliminated.

Conclusion

The purpose of interaction between subjects and objects is the creation of mature relationships within the structure of four position foundations. Every creation becomes complete through establishing harmonious relations with other beings in the formation of such foundations.

The energy that enables subjects and objects to give and receive in the creation of relationships is universal prime force, which comes from God. The foundation of this force and the life it sustains is the true love of God. The creation was made for love and it is only through the practice of true love that men and women can fulfill their potential as true human beings. The family unit is the four position foundation in which this human potential can be completely realized.

Given the ideal of true love and the four position foundation, what was God's purpose in creating the universe? What exactly is the role of human beings in the creation? How can men and women fulfill their purpose in life and become happy? These and related questions will be dealt with in the following chapter.

3 | THE PURPOSE OF CREATION

INTRODUCTION

The discussion of God and creation above shows that God's purpose is a unifying force that harmonizes His diverse creations within one, integrated and purposeful cosmos. But what exactly is that purpose? Why did God create? Since human beings were made in the image of God, and therefore are endowed with characteristics that mirror God's attributes, the key to answering this question is easily derived by understanding the fundamental motivation of humankind.

It is important to know God's purpose in making the creation because human beings can only fulfill their own purpose once they know clearly why God made them. Every being comes into existence to fulfill a purpose given to it by its creator: nothing creates itself or determines its own purpose. Consequently, a creation can only fulfill its potential by implementing its creator-given purpose. Since God is the Creator of all, His purpose for the creation is the creation's purpose.

It is the natural tendency of God's creations to carry out the purposes for which they were made. For example, hydrogen naturally combines with oxygen to form water; a lettuce plant unconsciously absorbs light, water and minerals in growing into food for human beings and animals; and, without having been shown how, a stork builds a nest to protect its eggs and young offspring until they can grow to take their place within the natural order.

Human beings, however, have free will, allowing them to choose to fulfill their given purpose. Free will is a gift from God that enables humankind to know and love God and participate with God in creative processes. If humans do not understand the purpose for which God made them, they are bound to make wrong choices and consequently live unfulfilled and tragic lives by failing to carry out their true purpose. However, when a person does fulfill his God-given purpose, he experiences complete joy and fulfillment.

The precise purpose for God making the creation and the way that purpose can be fulfilled by humanity and nature are discussed in this chapter.

Universal Human Purpose: Achieving True Happiness

The most universal human desire is for happiness. All men and women live to be happy, pursuing that aim as best they know how. Every action of every person is intended to increase his or her happiness. Even if pain is the immediate consequence of a decision to seek happiness, that pain is understood to be the price that must be paid to gain greater happiness. Thus an artist will make great efforts to create a substantial representation of his idea or vision, feeling joy once he has succeeded; an athlete will exhaust himself in training, driving his body to its limit so that he can experience the pleasure of achieving fitness and winning competitions; and a saint will live a life of sacrifice and hardship to gain the eternal joy of heaven.

How, then, is joy produced? When an object responds to the initiative of an appropriate subject, both are fulfilled and, for human beings, joy results. To return to the artist: he, as the subject, is happy when he succeeds in creating a work of art (object) that embodies his own ideas and therefore resembles him. The athlete experiences joy when his mind (subject) succeeds in getting his body (object) to respond fully to it in the achievement of sporting excellence. And the saint rejoices when his mind is able to gain complete mastery over his body in the service of God and other people. In each of these examples, joy is experienced when the body fulfills its purpose as an object to the mind by carrying out the instructions of the mind.

True happiness, or joy, is experienced only when human beings fulfill the purpose for which they were originally created. All other pursuits of happiness sooner or later lead to frustration and misery. Thus the individual who pursues his own happiness by exploiting the lives of others can never experience lasting joy. All moral and social crimes are of this nature: seeking happiness at the cost of other people's happiness. Action taken with a selfish and unrighteous motive always leads to the creation of human suffering, proving that it is contrary to humanity's true, God-endowed purpose.

The creation was made to complete itself through the formation of four position foundations based on giving and receiving between subjects and objects. It is when a subject and object form a harmonious union, centered on God's will, that each fulfills its purpose. Sub-atomic particles fulfill their purpose when they form atoms, atoms when they form molecules, and molecules when they form whole entities. Likewise, stamens and pistils fulfill their purpose when they cross-pollinate and produce seeds, and male and female animals when they mate and produce offspring.

In human society, this principle applies to all relationships, from the individual to the global. A child fulfills its purpose and is happy when it has harmonious relationships with its parents and siblings, while a mature man and woman fulfill their purpose and experience joy by adding to these existing relationships when they enter into a responsible, monogamous relationship of love, create children and raise a family. The happiness of children and parents produced by the giving and receiving of true love is the greatest human joy. Joy is also experienced in all other human relationships governed by true love, and hence centered on God's love. Giving and receiving love in a family is the model for giving and receiving love in society and among nations. In the family one learns the most essential truth: concern for the whole must be set above the interests of the individual.

Human experience shows that the degree of joy in a relationship depends on the compatibility of the characteristics and purposes of those involved. The most intense joy experienced by a woman is in the love relationship she has with the man who is her eternal mate. The couple's compatibility of purpose is total and the masculinity and femininity of the man and woman are perfectly complementary. When a man and woman unite in true love, their spiritual and physical natures fuse into one to create the highest joy for both partners. This demonstrates that man was made for woman and woman for man.

Individuals and families also experience joy in relating to other individuals, families, groups and nations, depending on mutuality of purpose. Social happiness is produced from harmonious relations among families, centered on God's love and truth; international happiness is produced from harmonious relations among nations, centered on God's will for those nations. The will of God is the purposeful expression of His love and truth.

Humans can also receive joy from their relationships with nature. Because nature was created in the image of human beings, as an environment to sustain them, men and women together encapsulate all the elements of the mineral, plant and animal kingdoms and are the only created beings that can relate to all other beings in the creation. The degree of resemblance between human and non-human beings determines the degree of joy experienced in the relationship. Pets, for example, generally demonstrate a high level of human-like characteristics, giving joy to the individuals who love them.

God Created to Experience Joy

God is the origin of all love, the First Lover. He is not distant from His creation, but intimately concerned with its welfare and development. Love, by its very nature, must be given, and therefore needs an object that can receive it. One cannot love nothing. God made the creation, centered on man and woman endowed with heart, as the object to receive His love. Without such an object, God would not be a God of love, but would remain a God of potential love. And without an object to whom He could give His love, God would not experience joy. Therefore, God made the creation, and in particular humankind, in order to experience joy through giving love.

It is because men and women were created by God for love that giving and receiving love is the central objective of their lives and the means by which they experience fulfillment and joy. Although God is perfect He seeks joy from His creation through the flowering of His love. His joy comes from experiencing men and women grow from infants through childhood into adulthood when, as mature parents, they create families, groups and nations living in the harmony created by relationships of true love. Their joy is His joy, their fulfillment His fulfillment.

Thus God seeks as much from His partners in the four position foundation as they seek from each other and from Him. Men and women are the culmination of creation, embodying the dual attributes of God more completely than any other beings. The high degree to which human beings resemble God, especially in their capacity to give and receive love, enables them to respond substantially to God and His love. God's Heart is essentially the heart of a parent for children and therefore the relationship between God and human beings can best be likened to a parent-child relationship.

Humans Were Created to Give Joy to God

God made human beings in such a way as to enable Him to experience joy through giving and receiving love with them. Consequently, the purpose of human life is to give joy to God. This is accomplished by perfecting human relationships to complete the four position foundation, centered on God. Men and women are endowed with heart and creativity, which are the attributes they need to complete the four position foundation and fulfill their purpose as objects of God's Heart and co-creators with God. When humans fulfill their God-given purpose, they feel complete and experience joy in giving joy to God. God's joy and human joy are inseparable.

Human beings were not created in a vacuum, but in a nurturing environment, which they need for the fulfillment of their purpose. God created the mineral, plant and animal kingdoms in the image of man and woman, to sustain and please human beings. The first man and woman were an encapsulation of all the cosmos created before them and for them, but they were unique in creation because they had both spirit and body, an internal character capable of communicating with God as well as an external form capable of communicating with the rest of creation. Mature men and women, who have become true parents, are the center of harmony between the invisible world of God and the visible world of nature. For this reason, God experiences joy in nature through human joy in nature.

The Three Blessings

In a complex world presenting men and women with multiple obligations, what are the essential steps they must take to fulfill their purpose? More specifically, what is it they must do to fulfill the four position foundation that gives joy to God?

Joy is produced when subject and object become one, resembling the oneness of God's attributes. The harmonization of subject and object creates beauty, which love seeks: love is attracted to the unified being of subject and object. Together, a harmonious subject and object represent a single object to love. Thus wherever love finds beauty, a subject finds its image in an object, joy is experienced by both subject and object in the giving and receiving between them. Since God created men and women out of His desire to give love and receive joy, human beings fulfill their purpose by becoming objects of beauty to God. In giving and receiving love with God, other humans and nature, men and women create beauty in all dimensions of their lives, experiencing joy and giving joy to God.

How can men and women become objects of beauty to God? They must become the image of God in their personalities and in their relations with other people and nature. They must complete four position foundations on all three levels, centered on God. By establishing these three foundations, human beings complete their purpose and qualify to receive the full blessing of God's true love. Hence these three foundations for the completion of human purpose are called *the three blessings*. To fulfill the three blessings, men and women must grow to become the image of God as mature individuals engaged in pure relationships within their families and the world, and exercise a dominion of true love over the rest of creation. In achieving these objectives, they come to mirror God and embody His beauty as true human beings.

The three blessings are: first, the ability and right (responsibility and potential) to become an individual with perfect personality and achieve the value of a complete, true being, sharing God's value; second, the ability and right to create an ideal family and world through fulfilling true love relationships, sharing God's ability to create new life and raise children; and, third, the ability and right to have dominion over the rest of creation, sharing God's capacity to make and modify things. By giving the three blessings, God shared his own perfect being fully with human beings, making them objects who can represent Him in the creation and reciprocate His love completely.

Fulfilling the three blessings is a process of growth and development in which an individual gradually discovers and understands who he or she is and how he himself, or she herself, functions and then learns how to relate to other people and nature. Through this process of self-discovery people learn about the laws that govern life and shape human nature, and, on this foundation, learn about the laws of relationship and, ultimately, the laws governing the whole universe. With this understanding they can truly inherit the creativity and lordship of God and fulfill their potential to have complete dominion over themselves and their environment and create relationships of joy and happiness in all circumstances.

The First Blessing

The first step towards becoming a true man or woman is taken by uniting mind and body, centered on God's will. The mind as subject, must have dominion over the body, its object. The body must learn to respond to the direction of the mind because the mind can understand and respond to God. The functions of the body, drinking, eating, moving, sleeping, procreating, and so on, are all to be directed by mind. Without the direction of mind, the body can take action that is contrary to the will of God, introducing impurity into an individual and making it difficult for God to relate to him and bless him. God can only have relationships with that in the creation which resembles Him. Without mutual resemblance, there is no common base for giving and receiving between God and creation.

Endowed with free will as an intrinsic part of their spiritual nature, men and women can choose to obey or disobey God. This means they can, through obedience, become the image of the selfless, loving and pure God, or, through disobedience, become self-ish and impure beings. Those who achieve mind-body unity centered on God become one with God's will and live in accordance with His word. Their words are one with God's truth and their actions are consistent with their words. They can be said to have godly personalities, and, filled with His love and truth, they are beautiful to Him. As true men and women, they fulfill *the first blessing.*

Through the first blessing, men and women establish the foundation for fulfilling the second and third blessings. They achieve this by becoming mature individuals who can think and feel like God and who have complete dominion over their own lives. In maturity, they would not deviate from the will of God because they share His purity of heart and would have no desire to violate true love. God's joy is their joy, God's pain their pain. This unity of love with God is the key to perfecting love in the family and society as well as love of all creation.

The Second Blessing

As children grow up to become adults, they learn how to give and receive love primarily at home, first in relations with their parents, then with brothers and sisters. The love learned at home prepares a man and woman to enter into mature conjugal love relations. Husband-wife love is the foundation for a married couple to have children and create a family. Through obedience to the will of God, a husband and wife create a relationship of true love, based on the true love of God. Their children are then born into a pure and God-centered home in which they are nurtured with true love so that they can grow into true men and women.

An infant lacks the capacity to know God directly. Only as it grows in spirit does it begin to develop a direct relationship with God. During that growing period, God is represented to the child by its parents, with the father embodying God's masculinity and the mother God's femininity. Thus, in a true love family, the children first come to experience the love and truth of God through the love and truth of their parents. For this reason, the personality of the parents (the relationship between their words and actions) is critically important to the development of their children. Only true parents, expressing God's love and truth through true personalities, can raise true children.

Children created in the image of God are true children. They are to grow through stages as true brothers and sisters to become true husbands and wives and, eventually, true parents themselves. The true families created in this process are the building blocks of a world governed by true love. The creation of true love clans, tribes and nations are stages in the building of a true world.

God's attributes, internal and external, masculine and feminine, are perfectly one within the divine nature so that when a man and woman, endowed with internal and external, male and female characteristics, become one in true love they come to resemble God fully. A family of pure love is the most beautiful object to God because it embodies the image of His own nature so totally. Consequently it can receive God's love in its most all-embracing and profound expressions. When a man and woman create a true love family, they fulfill *the second blessing*.

The Third Blessing

Human beings reach complete maturity in true families. The family unit not only embodies the image of God most completely, it also encapsulates the rest of creation. The union of man and woman in a true family is a microcosm of the perfection of all subject-object relationships throughout the universe, since the structures and functions of the bodies of men and women encapsulate the structures and functions of nature. Because human beings are a microcosm of the universe and the center of all natural hierarchies, true families can exercise God-centered dominion over nature, caring for the mineral, plant and animal kingdoms and, in return, being cared for by the creation. When families tend to nature with true love, they create a harmonious relationship between humankind and the rest of creation, a relationship of beauty that fulfills *the third blessing*.

Thus God's purpose for creating human beings is accomplished when they fulfill the conditions necessary to receive the three blessings. Men and women complete their purpose by earning all three blessings.

Universal Human Aspirations

Although not articulated in the same terminology, the essential aims of all religions and ethical systems are encompassed within the three blessings, which, in terms of human fulfillment, represent the aspirations of all people. There is no one, whether a religious person or not, who would not like to be a whole, fulfilled individual living in perfect love within a joyful family and peaceful world and existing in harmony with nature.

Human misery and suffering increase in direct proportion to an individual's distance from achieving these basic objectives. It is no exaggeration to say that all human ills, the hatreds, crimes, conflicts, injustices and oppression that characterize this troubled world, derive from the misshapen lives of men and women who fail to fulfill the conditions to receive the three blessings: individuals who cannot unite mind and body create families lacking in true love and become people who are abusive of other human beings and nature.

Restoring The World Begins With Individuals

The existence of huge contradictions between God's ideal and the reality of the world known to humans implies that there has been a massive human failure to fulfill the purpose of creation. (The nature of this failure is explained in Chapter 7.) By understanding the three blessings, it is clear that the path leading this sickly world back to health begins with the restoration of individuals. Only true men and women can create good families and a peaceful world of true love.

One can think of the world's problems as instances of the human body unrighteously taking dominion over the mind. This is the root of all materialism, which sets the value of the external, physical world of the body above the internal, spiritual world of the mind. The evident global disorder was produced by disorder in nations, societies, tribes and families, made up of disordered people. At root, then, the key to solving the world's problems lies in solving the mind-body relationship within individuals. Restored individuals can build restored families and then restore all other human relationships. They can also restore the human relationship with nature. For this reason, the history of God's work to restore fallen humanity to the original ideal has focused on finding one man and one woman who can become true parents and fulfill the original purpose for humankind by realizing the three blessings.

The Mission of Religion

Preparation of the world for this central providence of God has been the mission of the world's religions. They have all encouraged individuals to unite mind and body centered on the will of God, or altruistic principles at one with God's will. Religion recognizes that the root of all evils is to be found in individuals and therefore the cure for humankind must begin with individual purification and restoration. The essential message of religion is that when the mind gains dominion over the body (the first blessing), the other goals of life (the second and third blessings) can be achieved. Religion educates human beings to fulfill the three blessings, teaching the virtues of individual faith and purity, the sanctity of family and respect for nature. In sum, the mission of religion is to educate people how to fulfill the three blessings in preparation to receive the messianic true parents, who are the first couple to completely fulfill the ideal of God's creation, and therefore the model for all other people to emulate.

Conclusion

God made the creation as an object to which He could give His love and from which He could receive joy. For God and humanity, joy is produced when an object comes to resemble a subject and enters into a harmonious relationship with it. Men and women were created to give joy to God, which they can do by growing to resemble Him, in harmony with other people and with nature, fulfilling three blessings. The failure of humankind to fulfill the three blessings is the fundamental problem that underlies all the problems of this world. The solution to these problems lies, then, in the restoration of the three blessings, beginning with one man and one woman who can create a true family as the foundation for a true world.

The three blessings are not achieved in an instant, but as the fruit of a process of growth. As the body needs time to reach physical maturity, so too the mind needs time to reach spiritual maturity. The principles that govern the process of growth to maturity are discussed in the next chapter.

4 | THE GROWING PROCESS

INTRODUCTION

The three blessings are achieved in the context of a universal principle: nothing begins existence in its completed form; rather, every being achieves maturity through a process of growth and development. Mature human beings, with all their sophistication and multiple capabilities, start life as a single fertilized cell, develop into the infant form of a man or woman in the womb and then enter the physical world to grow to adulthood in a process that takes many years.

What are the principles that govern growth? What is the relationship between physical and spiritual growth? What are the similarities and differences between the growing processes for human beings and for other beings in the creation? How can spiritual growth be measured? This chapter examines these issues.

Three Stages of Growth

There are three fundamental stages in the growing period: *formation, growth* and *completion*. Only by completing three stages of growth can a being fulfill its proper place in the order of creation. The three stages are derived from the process of creation itself, in which all things come into being through the three-step development of the four position foundation: 1. God originates all creations as the First Cause of all being; 2. God manifests as two divided but complementary entities, the subject and object; and 3. subject and object interact to produce a new oneness and a new creation.

Three represents completion in the creation. For example, nature is divided into three kingdoms: animal, vegetable and mineral; the physical world exists in three primary states: solid, liquid and gas; and the many hues that adorn the creation are derived from three primary colors: red, yellow and blue. Two-dimensional space is created by a minimum of three points; three-dimensional space by a minimum of three lines; all physical objects exist in three dimensions; and three points are the minimum needed to support any object.

Growth in Nature's Kingdoms

In nature's three kingdoms the three stages of growth are apparent. In the inorganic mineral kingdom, the structures that make up the physical world are built in three stages: sub-atomic particles (formation), atoms (growth) and molecules (completion). In the organic plant and animal kingdoms, living entities reach maturity through three stages of growth. For example, a plant begins life as a seed which contains the biological blueprint for the development of an oak tree, rose or cabbage. In the formation stage the seed sprouts into an initial form of the completed plant, in the growth stage it takes on the plant's mature form and in the completion stage it produces seeds from which new plants spring, completing the cycle of growth.

Animals begin life as fertilized eggs, or zygotes, which are encoded with the biological instructions for a mature creature. In the formation stage of its development, an animal becomes an embryonic miniature of what it will be on completion. It begins the growth stage by graduating from its gestation period (a calf is born and a chick hatched, for example) to develop into a mature being. After completing the final stage of growth it mates and produces offspring. The growth cycle then begins anew.

The Growth of Human Beings

Because of their spiritual nature, human beings follow a different course of growth than that of other beings. As essentially spiritual beings endowed with free will, their growth is the result of interaction between the spirit and body, a process of development controlled by human will, according to God's principles of growth. The body passes through a cycle of growth that parallels that of certain animals, but as it grows so too must the spirit. Once the body has completed its work and dies, the invisible but mature spirit continues to exist in the non-physical realm. For humankind, the purpose of physical growth during the limited life span of the body is to nurture development of the eternal human spirit.

There are three fundamental stages of human life. First, an embryo develops in the womb; second, the physical and spiritual elements grow to full maturity in the physical world; and, finally, the physical body dies and the eternal spirit embarks on its discarnate existence in the spiritual world. The three stages of life are linked by dramatic death and birth transitions: the first when life in the womb ends with the death of the placenta and the birth of an infant man or woman into life on earth; the second when life on earth ends with the death of the physical body and 'birth' of the spirit into the spirit world. This physical-to-spiritual evolution embraces two inter-related growing processes, one physical, one spiritual.

The Physical Growth of Humans

The life of the physical body also has three stages: gestation in the womb (in trimesters); growth to full maturity on earth (in three seven-year periods); and a final period of multiplication and enjoyment of the three blessings before the body dies and the spirit continues by itself in the spirit world.

The key period of growth is the first 21 years following the birth of a baby. Although a baby begins life on earth with distinct male or female features and all vital organs, it only develops into a fully mature human being, capable of reproduction and true dominion over the rest of creation, during the first two decades of its existence on earth. By the end of adolescence, the body is fully equipped to carry out the desires of the mind, according to the will of God. This means it is capable of carrying out all the functions associated with completing the three blessings. The three seven-year periods of this growing process represent the formation, growth and completion stages of physical maturation.

The Spiritual Growth of Humans

The life of a human spirit begins with the birth of a baby. The spirit man or woman grows through three stages, in parallel with the physical body, reaching full spiritual maturity by the age of 21. To be fully mature, the spirit must respond perfectly to God's love and live by God's absolute standard of beauty, truth and goodness. By developing his capacity to receive and give love, first as a child, then a sibling and finally a spouse and parent, an individual completes his spiritual growth.

The Principles of Growth

Humankind's natural environment grows through the autonomous power of the principles of creation. Given the elements required for growth, plants and animals pass through three stages of development to reach maturity, as described above, guided by natural laws created by God. Animals and plants, lacking a spiritual nature, do not consciously participate in their own growing processes: God endowed their internal characters with instructions and instincts which guide them automatically to fulfillment according to the purposes for which they were made. The same holds true for the physical bodies of human beings. Given the necessary elements, sunlight and air, food and drink, men and women grow naturally to full physical maturity, becoming physically capable of reproduction and taking dominion over nature and all material things.

The Indirect Dominion of Law

Human beings are not only physical, however. They have a spiritual nature as well as a body, an inner being through which they are linked with God and other people. Since this internal mind of human beings governs their entire identity and life, it's growth to maturity is ultimately more important than the growth of the physical body. What then is spiritual growth and how is it achieved?

Since humankind was made to receive and reciprocate God's love, the most important purpose for men and women is learning how to give and receive true love. Essentially, growth of the spirit is growth in capacity to give and receive pure love. This development of love is what enables men and women to resemble God and fulfill the three blessings. In the formation stage, a child begins this process by receiving love from its parents and older brothers and sisters, complemented by the love from relatives and friends of the family. The child expresses a passive love in responding to the love it receives. As it grows, it learns to give as well as receive in the intimate circle of its family, eventually developing the capacity for mutual love. On this foundation of fully mature love, a man and woman are prepared to enter into a relationship of conjugal love and take full responsibility for children, giving them unconditional parental love.

The growth of love is accomplished through obedience to God's law. Before an individual is fully mature, he must be guided by instructions from God so that he does not misuse his capacity to love. It is the role of parents to communicate the laws of true love to their children, through word and deed. Children who grow into men and women learning how to love according to God's principles live virtuous lives and fulfill the purpose of their creation. True parents are fully qualified to guide their children to maturity and fulfillment of the three blessings. In particular, the father and mother, with the wisdom and compassion of true parental love, know when a child has reached the level of maturity to enter into a relationship of conjugal love and become a parent, and can provide the best advice in selection of a spouse.

Love is a spontaneous expression of heart. It cannot be programed into a person or forced from him. It must be freely given, and received. For this reason, God created human beings with free will, which is the nature to make conscious choices. Humans learn to give and receive true love by learning to make the right choices in life. Just as a child needs to study and internalize the rules of mathematics or language to become a master in those fields, so too he needs to master the rules of love to become mature in its practice. Once heart is perfected through this maturation process, all its expressions of love flow freely and spontaneously in accordance with the rules of true love.

Since God is the source of all love, the rules of true love are His. Any expression of love in contravention of His rules is false love. The rules of true love are the basis for God's laws, or principles. It is these laws, together with corrective instructions for disobedient people, that are variously articulated by the world's religions, as, for example, in the Ten Commandments given to Moses, the Sermon on the Mount of Jesus and the Five Pillars of Islam in the teaching of Mohammed. All religious laws derive from one: human beings should not misuse the love of God. Described metaphorically in both the Bible and the Koran, this is the only law God gave to the first man and woman, Adam and Eve. They were told they were free to enjoy the Garden of Eden to its full, with one caution: they were not allowed to partake of the fruit of a particular tree. This prohibition meant they were warned, at the cost of their lives, not to engage in illicit love. (A full explanation of the scriptural accounts is given in Chapter 7.)

The rules of love have to be articulated because people are born immature and have to pass through a learning process, guided by the laws of God, to reach maturity. Therefore, to cultivate true love and grow to completion, individuals must exercise their free will in obedience to the laws of God.

God's laws contain the directions that people must follow to reach the goal of full maturity, but in starting life as infants, men and women cannot comprehend such laws and have no knowledge of God at all. For this reason, the role of parents is vital. Embodying the parenthood of God, true parents live with the love and by the laws of God, such that their children learn about the nature of God and the practice of His love and laws as a natural part of their growing experience. A boy initially grows in the image of his father, and a girl in the image of her mother. Only once they are intellectually and emotionally developed can a man and woman understand and obey the laws of God directly.

Until men and women have completed the three stages of growth, they remain only partial images of God. This means that the communication between God and humanity during the growing period is limited by human immaturity, very much as the relationship between mature parents and their children is limited by the immaturity of the children. As the children grow in understanding and love, their relationship with their parents deepens and broadens. So it is with God and humankind.

The goal of human growth is to achieve oneness with God: full compatibility of heart and love. In that stage of being, human love will be true love, in the image of God's true love, and human actions will be completely at one with God's will. To reach that goal, men and women must obey the word, or laws, of God. During the period of human growth, when God relates to human beings through the mediation of His laws, individuals remain in the *indirect dominion* of God: they are not yet completely accessible and responsive to God.

Responsibility and Freedom

The special position of human beings in the creation carries with it special blessings and special responsibilities. In particular, as co-creators with God, humans have their own portion of responsibility in seeing that God's original plan for the creation is carried out. Men and women exercise their co-creatorship by contributing their efforts to their own perfection and the fulfillment of the three blessings. Therefore, it is the responsibility of human beings to obey the word of God out of their own volition. If they do not obey God, they will be unable to grow to maturity and God's ideal will not be realized.

Once humans have fulfilled their responsibility, they are completely free, that is they are not limited in making choices because all the options they might consider would be within the province of God's will and, therefore, result in goodness. Conversely, there is no true freedom without responsibility. Anyone who makes choices in contradiction to his or her obligations to God will act in violation of His principles and bring about destruction of His ideal. Hence evil in the world is caused by an abuse of free will: men and women exercising their God-given freedom in disobedience to God.

Thus although God provides the natural environment for human physical growth, as well as the love and laws needed for spiritual growth, it is the response of individuals to God that determines their destiny. What a person contributes to his own completion is just a small part of what is needed for human development (God gives the rest), but it is the key to fulfillment of God's purpose for human beings. Therefore the primary mission of human life is the fulfillment of human responsibility through obedience to God's will.

The Direct Dominion of Love

God's law is a guide for giving and receiving love. When humans obey God's instructions, they mature in their love to the point where their love resembles God's true love and they can enter into the *direct dominion* of God's love, in which the bond of love between God and humankind precludes any disobedient desire in men and women. God's will and human will become one, such that human desire is only to please God. Thus the goal of human life and the object of growth is to exist in perfect union with God and be obedient to Him out of mature love. (People bring fear of retribution and punishment on themselves when they are disobedient to God.) This is the ideal of a parent-child relationship, in which the child obeys its parent out of love and affection and not fear. The three blessings can only be completely fulfilled when individuals enter the direct dominion of God, creating families and nations maintained in perfect harmony with His will and secured by unbreakable bonds of true love.

Conclusion

As with all created beings, humans grow through three stages to reach maturity. Human growth differs from that of minerals, plants and animals in that it contains a spiritual element that transcends and gives purpose to the physical. The object of human life is the perfection of love for the completion of the three blessings. Once an individual has reached full physical and spiritual maturity, completing the first blessing, he or she is qualified to create a true love family and take dominion over creation, fulfilling the second and third blessings.

Human growth to maturity on earth is preparation for an eternal existence in the spirit world. The nature of this invisible world and its relationship to the physical world known to our five physical senses is the topic of the next chapter.

5 | THE PHYSICAL WORLD AND THE SPIRITUAL WORLD

INTRODUCTION

Previous chapters have discussed the dual nature of the creation, the fact that it has internal character as well as external form, positive and negative elements. The internal character is invisible to the physical senses and yet it is responsible for the behavior of the external reality that is observed by humans. The implication of this is that the invisible inner world of creation is causal and therefore more important than the world known to human senses. And yet so little is known about this internal dimension of reality. This is due, in part, to the fact that its study has remained the province of religion, which is the object of considerable skepticism in the modern, scientific world. Nevertheless, science itself recognizes the existence of invisible, causal forces that are only recognized through the impact they have on the observable world.

The realm of invisible, causal reality need not remain shrouded in mystery. Indeed, there is an urgent need for humanity to develop a comprehensive understanding of life's inner dimensions in order to put human existence on earth into proper perspective and order. Rampant materialism, which threatens the cultural foundations of society, will continue unchecked unless men and women learn to balance the concerns of their transient existence on earth with the everlasting values of eternal existence in the spiritual world.

This chapter explains the existence of the spiritual world and its relationship to the physical world, in particular the pivotal role of human beings who are endowed with spiritual nature and created to be the center of harmony between the physical and spiritual worlds. It answers the questions: what is the nature of the spiritual world? How does it relate to the physical world? How do human beings mediate between the two worlds? How does the human spirit grow? Where does an individual's spirit go when he dies? What are Hell, Paradise and Heaven?

The Physical World and Spiritual World

The *physical world*, which is known to humans through their five physical senses, is complemented by an invisible *spiritual world*, or simply spirit world, known to humans through their five spiritual senses. This is not a world of fantasy or imagination but a completely real environment for the human spirit, which is itself invisible.

The reality of the spirit world can best be understood by recognizing the reality of intangible forces in life, such as the power of love to influence people through the invisible bonds of family, friendship, nationality, race and religion. It is fair to say that most peoples' lives are governed by invisible forces of belief, relationship, tradition and culture. The physical world of humanity's environment is shaped by these internal forces because the activities of the body are directed by the mind. The realm of mind and spirit is causal to the world of body.

Because humanity is presently separated from God, resulting in a dysfunctional relationship between the spiritual and physical parts of human beings, there are few people who are truly conscious of the spirit world and how it operates. And yet it is the place where all humanity is destined to live for eternity after passing from the physical world upon the death of the body.

The Physical Person and Spiritual Person

So far, this text has only spoken of human dual characteristics of mind and body, but the concept of mind and body needs elaboration into a more comprehensive and accurate description of the internal and invisible nature of human beings and how it relates to the external and visible person. Human beings have two parts: the *spirit person* and *physical person*, or simply the spirit and body.

The physical person is created at conception and continues to live until physical death; the spirit person begins its autonomous existence at the birth of a baby. It exists forever, first connected to the physical person, and then, once the spirit is mature and the body dies, in the spiritual world, detached from the physical world.

The spirit person has both a spirit mind, the seat of the human desire for joy and the source of emotion, intellect and will, and a spirit body, which responds to the desires of his spiritual mind. The spirit person is completely substantial in the sense that it has a distinct shape (visible to the spiritual eyes of others) and functions much like the physical person, without the limitations of time and space. The physical person has a physical mind, which operates through the brain and central nervous system, and a physical body, which responds to the desires of his physical mind.

The human mind, then, essentially is an invisible, spiritual aspect of humans that is subject over the physical person and provides direction and purpose to human existence. In an individual alive physically, the physical mind interacts with the spirit mind to create the human mind, the causal aspect of his being. Through perfection of the spirit mind–physical mind relationship, the human mind is completed as *original mind*. Once the physical body dies, the physical mind ceases to function but the original mind exists forever, maintaining an eternal relationship with the spiritual body.

The spiritual mind is the core of the spirit person, controlling the eternal life, love and ideals of individuals. Through it, human existence gains value as emotion, intellect and will pursue, respectively, beauty, truth and goodness. It is the place in humans where God can dwell. The physical mind is similar to an animal's instinct, manifesting desires for nourishment, self-protection, comfort and reproduction, thereby maintaining the life of the body.

In an ideal state, the strong desires of the physical person are naturally object to even stronger desires of the spirit person, and harmonized through the perfection of the mind-body relationship. Only when people are separated from God through disobedience and sin, and consequently their minds are dominated by their bodies in an inversion of the first blessing, can human desires create the type of chaos and suffering seen in the world today where rampant physical lusts are pursued at the cost of spiritual values.

The *conscience* exists to guide people towards a proper relationship between spirit and body. The conscience is the interaction of the spiritual mind with the physical mind during the formation of original mind. The conscience directs humans towards fulfillment of their true purpose as beings of absolute value, guiding them according to their levels of maturity. Only original mind can fully comprehend absolute values of beauty, truth and goodness and thus direct humanity in a life of perfect oneness with God. In the fallen world relative standards prevail, hence the diversity in moral codes and ethical systems. It is the role of religion to educate the human mind to develop ever more accurate and profound understanding of absolute values, going beyond the limitations of relative standards. In this way religious truth serves as the basis for the working of conscience. The more human mind becomes original mind, the closer the conscience comes to directing people according to absolute standards of beauty, truth and goodness.

The Mission of the Body

The physical world was created by God to sustain physical bodies. But the body has a limited life span, during which it must accomplish two vital functions: it must nurture the spirit from infancy to full maturity; and it must facilitate the multiplication of spirit men and women through human reproduction. In performing these functions, the body enables human beings to realize their fundamental purpose and desire: to experience joy through the fulfillment of the three blessings. To accomplish its mission, the body itself is designed to experience physical joy, or pleasure.

Once the 'mission' of the body has been accomplished, it dies and returns to earth, where it disintegrates into its basic elements, never to exist as a whole again. As the body dies, the spirit departs from it and embarks on life in the spiritual world in its eternal, discarnate state. The spirit is fully equipped for life in the spiritual world, having attributes that enable it to interact with other spirit men and women as well as the spiritual counterparts to the physical world of nature. Paralleling the five senses of the body, the spirit body has sight, hearing, smell, taste and touch, with which it can know and enjoy the spiritual world.

There are a few people on earth who have their spiritual senses finely developed, in tune with their bodily senses, such that they are able to perceive and interact with the spiritual world at will. Many of these men and women are deeply religious, while others find themselves in possession of these abilities but don't attribute any particular significance to them. A third group uses its access to the spiritual world for selfish purposes, in negative forms of witchcraft, voodoo and the like.

Growth of the Spirit

Men and women grow to maturity through the interaction between the spirit and body, each of which takes in elements for growth from the other as well as from sources outside the human being. For the body, growth is achieved by taking in external elements from sunlight, air, food and drink as well as internal elements from the spirit. For the spirit, growth comes from receiving internal elements from God's love and truth as well as external elements from the body. The fundamental objective of spiritual growth is the perfection of love through three stages of maturation within the family (passive, mutual and unconditional love), as described in the previous chapter.

In the growing process, the body provides the spirit with energy called *vitality elements.* Doing good deeds generates good vitality elements, whereas doing wrong produces evil vitality elements. The spirit needs good vitality elements to grow. People feel good when they do good, but, conversely, feel bad when they disobey God, because the spirit recognizes the quality of vitality elements it receives and reacts favorably to good and unfavorably to bad elements. In the same way that an unhealthy diet damages the body, bad vitality elements damage the spirit. Thus the spirit of a person who has lived an evil life is literally ugly.

The spirit gives energy to the body as *spirit elements*. When inspired by love and truth, the spirit generates spirit elements that energize the body to do good. When, on the other hand, the spirit is itself cut off from God's love and truth, it is deprived of spiritual energy, preventing growth of the spirit. The effect of this lack of spiritual life is to stop the flow of spirit elements to the body. This is the equivalent of starvation: without food the body cannot grow. Worse than starving the body, though, is giving it poison. The spiritual equivalent of poison is evil spirit elements, passed to the body when the spirit has relations with evil spirits and is influenced by falsehood and hatred.

Vitality and spirit elements are exchanged between body and spirit such that the internal character and external activities of a person always go hand in hand. A good life is built on good deeds, inspired by love and truth. Since love and truth originate with God, and are given to human beings as the *life element*, in an ideal world they would naturally flow to individuals at one in heart with God. In the human state of disobedience and separation from God, however, religion exists to facilitate the flow of life elements. The essence of a religious life is the pursuit of love and truth. But God's love and truth can flow to men and women only to the extent that they share them with others through the dissemination of truth and the performance of good deeds. Receiving has to be reciprocated by giving, or the flow of love and truth is blocked and growth of the spirit is stunted. Through a life of study, contemplation, meditation and prayer, balanced by service to humanity, a man or woman of God grows in spiritual maturity. The greater the love and truth received from God, the greater the virtue of that person's words and deeds, and the greater the stimulation of the spirit, enabling it to increase its capacity to receive yet more of God's life element.

Ignorance or denial of God does not prevent the interaction of vitality and spirit elements, but it severely limits the scope for human growth. The life element, which comes from God, is the source of life and subject over the spirit and vitality elements. It operates whether or not individuals recognize its existence, but ignorance of it prevents people from using it to maximum effect. This condition can be illustrated by the example of pre-industrial people living in ignorance of electricity and consequently existing without any of the benefits of that great energy source: they got shocked by static and lightning but lacked electric lighting and household appliances. Ignorance of God is, ultimately, devastating because it condemns humans to existence in a state of partial completion wherein they can never fulfill their true purpose or achieve complete relationships.

In the original creation of God, the human body and spirit would have grown to maturity in parallel, within the same time period, so that there would exist a perfect balance between them. In the world as it is, however, there is generally a huge discrepancy between the physical and spiritual development of human beings. Given the necessary physical elements, all bodies grow to completion, but spirits, distant from God, are not able to reach maturity. This discordance between spirit and body is responsible for the evils of humankind. In a person with a mature body but immature spirit the natural order of creation, in which the mind takes the subject position over the body, is reversed, and the body, which is ignorant of God, initiates actions that are destructive to the spirit. (When one speaks of the body usurping the subject role of the mind, in fact one is describing a reversal of priorities in the mind itself, such that the needs of the physical being are placed above the needs of the spiritual being, contrary to the order of God's creation. In this state, people lose their value as a human beings, since it is the spirit that makes humans unique and central in creation.)

A spiritually sensitive person can distinguish the level of spiritual maturity in another person, and even ordinary people can normally sense the changes in character and attitudes that accompany changes in the levels of the vitality and spirit elements given and received between the spirit and body. An insincere smile cannot disguise a low spirit for long, while the goodness of even the most humble person will sooner or later shine through, irrespective of external circumstances.

Hell, Paradise and Heaven

The true beauty (or ugliness) of a person's spirit is determined by his or her relationship with God, and is reflected directly in spiritual appearance: higher spirits are brighter than lower spirits. Love is the source of spiritual light and warmth. Wherever human beings make a base for God's love to be present, by creating four position foundations centered on God, there is spiritual light and warmth.

The spiritual level at which a person begins life in the spiritual world is determined by the level achieved while on earth. Upon the death of a body, there is no magical transformation of character whereby certain chosen individuals are absolved of their responsibilities and elevated to Heaven while others are damned to lives of eternal misery in Hell. Spirits exist at all levels of growth. *Hell*, the spiritual realm below the formation stage, is where *evil spirits* are found, whereas the formation stage is populated with *form spirits*. The growth stage opens the realm of *Paradise*, which is for *life spirits*. Having passed through the completion stage, life spirits finally become *divine spirits* as they enter the direct dominion of God's love, which is the realm of *Heaven*. Evil spirits are the most distant from God, existing in gross violation of His principles and manifesting ugliness, falsehood and evil instead of beauty, truth and goodness. The level of a spirit when the body dies is the level at which it embarks on life in the spirit world.

Since the body is needed to provide vitality elements for growth of the spirit, the growing process is to be carried out on earth until spiritual maturity is achieved. Men and women who do not reach the completion stage on earth have to continue their efforts to grow as disembodied spirits by cooperating with people on earth. This is unimaginably more difficult than growing while on earth, since on earth an individual has a body to give vitality elements to his spirit directly. Once detached from his body, a person can only gain the benefits of vitality elements faintly and indirectly, by serving righteous men and women still on earth.

In the ideal world of God's creation, there is no Hell, and everybody enjoys life in the beautiful realm of Heaven after reaching oneness with God. Heavenly life would be achieved on earth and then continued in the spirit world after the body dies. There would be no need to fear death (as so many do today because of their distance from God and ignorance of the spiritual world) because the end of life on earth would be the beginning of a more beautiful and joyful existence in the spirit world. At birth, a child enters a vastly greater and more resplendent world than its mother's womb. Likewise, when physical death frees a spirit from the body, the spirit man enters a world of much greater diversity and beauty than the physical world. However, this spirit world can only be enjoyed to the extent the spirit person is mature in love, in the same way that the physical world can only be fully enjoyed by men and women whose bodies are whole and mature.

Conclusion

To gain an accurate perspective on life, human beings need to understand the invisible spiritual world, which is the world they were created to live in forever. Life on earth is preparation for eternal life in the spiritual world. Because the body is a microcosm of the physical world and the spirit a microcosm of the spiritual world, humans stand at the center of creation. Without harmony between spirit and body there cannot be harmony between the spiritual and physical worlds. The growth of the spirit and body to full maturity creates that harmony, and once the three blessings have been completed the mission of the body is accomplished. Whatever is left unaccomplished of this earthly purpose must be completed in the spiritual world after the body dies. The people of this world, past and present, in the spirit world and on earth, exist at various levels of maturity.

In the world that God originally created all men and women were to achieve the perfection of their spiritual beings while on earth. Why then are people spiritually incomplete and immature? And why is the history of humankind so filled with evil of all sorts, hatred, enmity, aggression, oppression, violence and wars, instead of love, as intended by God?

Clearly something has gone seriously wrong. The world as it is does not resemble the world of God's ideal. Free will is not exercised responsibly and people do anything to satisfy their selfish desires, in the process destroying the beauty and goodness of God's creation.

The first part of this book has laid out a scenario for a good, God-centered world, free from the evils that now bedevil humankind. The ideal described is not a fantasy, but rather the world that God intended when He made the creation. It can and must be realized in time because God's will for His creation is absolute. The second part, which follows, explains why there is such a huge discrepancy between the world of God's ideal and the reality that exists today. Although the human fall is accepted by the three monotheistic religions, it needs to be understood in the light of what has been presented here so far, in particular the importance of human responsibility. Once that is clear, a basis exists for understanding God's work to restore fallen humanity, which is explained in the third and final part.

6 | PREDESTINATION

INTRODUCTION

A fundamental paradox of religion is that although God, the creator of all things, is almighty and good, the world people live in and know through history is full of evil. In other words, the sinful world of human experience does not mirror the sinless, perfect God who created it.

This paradox is further complicated by the widely-held belief that an omniscient and omnipotent God must be in control of all human affairs and thus predetermines the course of human lives and history. Taken to its extreme, this traditional theory of predestination obviates the need for human effort altogether, including the practice of prayer, meditation, fasting and other religious disciplines, since an individual's destiny is decided by God irrespective of his thoughts and deeds. But if God is in full control of human destiny, why are human lives, past and present, so steeped in ungodliness? How could it be that a good and loving God created a world of sin and suffering?

The key to resolving this seeming contradiction lies in understanding why God gave a portion of responsibility to His children, according to which human destiny is determined both by the will of God and individuals' voluntary response to God's will. If human beings fail in their portion of responsibility, the fulfillment of God's will is postponed until such time as they become responsible. An individual's life is predestined for goodness by God, but the fulfillment of that purpose depends on his or her response to God.

Love and Free Will

As discussed in Chapter 3, men and women were created to receive love from God and to return love to Him by sharing it with others within the paradigm of the three blessings. Love can only be given and received out of human free will. Any human expressions of affection and passion that are forced or contrary to God's will are not in fact true love, but merely simulations of it. They cannot truly fulfill men and women and they do not give joy to God.

It is the essence of God's nature to give love. God's desire to experience joy by giving and receiving love inspired the creation of a man and woman to receive and reciprocate His love. But God would not force His children to respond to Him and His love because to do so would violate His own principles of love, principles by which God exists and by which He created. Therefore human beings are free to love God or not to love Him.

God did not create human beings with the expectation that they would love from birth. They were made to grow in their capacity to receive and give love, passing through the three stages of the learning process: formation, growth and completion. Thus God created His children with only one purpose and destiny: to grow to maturity as true men and women who would develop their love in the creation of families, tribes, nations and a world of true love relationships, centered on God. This purpose is unchanging and absolute, a manifestation of God's absolutely good nature. Therefore, it is right to believe that human destiny on the individual, family, tribal, national and global levels is predetermined to be one of goodness and ultimate fulfillment.

Human Responsibility

However, the timing of the fulfillment of humanity's original, good destiny is determined by the response of individuals to God, in particular the fulfillment of their responsibility to learn how to give and receive love. Until human beings fulfill that responsibility, they will not be fulfilled and will not create the world of love and goodness that God intended.

It is not in any way a diminution of God's power for Him to endow His creation with a portion of responsibility. On the contrary, to do so is to confirm His omnipotence in that all His creation ultimately lies within His domain and belongs to Him. Regardless of what people do with God's gifts to them, eventually God's will shall be done. The unchanging will of God is for human beings to create an ideal world by completing the three blessings.

Thus the traditional view of predestination, namely that all things (including human salvation and damnation) are predetermined by God as part of His overall scheme for the creation, is correct in recognizing the absolute nature of God and His will, but wrong in ignoring the role of human beings in the accomplishment of that will. Without understanding the human portion of responsibility in salvation, the traditional belief in predestination provides a theological basis for individuals to maintain a fatalistic view of life instead of a responsible attitude towards God, other people and nature. Traditional predestination also negates the value of religious figures who have appeared in history as guides and saviors for fallen humans, begging the question: if the destiny of men and women is pre-determined, why would God send prophets and messengers to turn fallen people from ways of error to paths of goodness?

Conclusion

The evil that exists in the world today, and has made human history such a tragic record, is not part of God's dispensation for humanity, but rather the product of men and women failing their responsibilities. Not until people take full responsibility for their lives will evil end and good begin. All people are predestined to live lives of goodness, in the fulfillment of God's ideal, but the timing of that fulfillment depends on them. To believe that human life is determined by God's will alone can lead to irresponsibility and fatalism, whereas to recognize and carry out the human portion of responsibility in the fulfillment of God's will leads to a life of spiritual growth and the completion of human purpose.

The next chapter will show how the first man and woman failed to fulfill their responsibilities, and how this affected fulfillment of

their predestined purposes. Instead of completing the three blessings, they destroyed the ideal world intended by God and created
Hell instead of Heaven. Their error is the root cause of all that has
been wrong in human history and all that is wrong in the world today.

In the aftermath of their failure, God's predestined will for humankind had to be fulfilled by the descendants of the first human
ancestors, in particular central figures chosen by God to establish
models of human responsibility in response to His commandments.

PART
II

THE HUMAN
FALL

INTRODUCTION

God's ideal for the creation, as outlined in Part One, was never realized. Neither in history nor in the present-day world can one find the ideal world God intended when he created humankind and nature. Why is this? Why is there such a dramatic contradiction between God's ideal and the reality of the world?

These questions are addressed in Part Two of the Principle, which is comprised of three chapters. These chapters explain the mission of the first man and woman, Adam and Eve; how they responded to that mission; and what the results of their actions were for their family and all humanity. This subject is called the human fall because it discusses the process by which the original man and woman lost their privileged places in creation and were separated from God's love by their own disobedience.

Once God's ideal and the fall are clearly understood, a foundation exists for analyzing the history of restoration, the process by which God has been working to restore fallen humanity to its original position.

7 | THE HUMAN FALL

INTRODUCTION

There is no denying that our world is far from the ideal of God's original purpose for the creation. Instead of being populated by happy and prosperous individuals living in harmonious families within a peaceful global community, the world is torn asunder by conflicts at all levels. Typically, life is an exercise in frustration and unfulfilled hopes that offers only occasional glimpses of a joyful and satisfying existence. Anyone who tries to do good finds himself confronted by strong opposing forces, both from the unprincipled aspect of his own nature as well as from evils within society. The struggle between good and evil that characterizes human activity on earth is the result of battles between good and evil within individuals.

Human history has seen some improvements in life on the external level, but these developments have been achieved against a background of unending war and bloodshed and unreconciled divisions between individuals, families, tribes and nations. The supreme efforts of the best men and women of history have failed to resolve the internal and external conflicts of humanity. And yet the God of true love could not have predestined humankind to live in a world of suffering and misery. What went wrong? What happened to God's ideal? How did human beings come to be at war with themselves, other people and nature? Why is it so difficult for humans to live the life of goodness they were made for? The Bible and Koran offer specific accounts of the origin of evil in the first human beings, Adam and Eve, but these are symbolic stories of the human fall. Nevertheless, when properly interpreted, they reveal a real history of the original human separation from God which is the source of archetypes that characterize fallen relations in history and the world today. By understanding the meaning behind scriptural symbols, one can unlock the secrets of human sin and suffering and recognize the nature of the solution needed to restore humanity. This chapter offers an explanation of the human fall based on the Principle.

The Origin of Evil and Satan

Before a doctor can prescribe treatment to cure a patient's illness, he must correctly diagnose the sickness. Likewise, before humans can rid the world of evil, they must discover evil's origin and learn how to eliminate it. Furthermore, to meet the requirements of science and religion, a satisfactory explanation of evil must provide a true analysis of the root cause of human separation from God and the sinful behavior that causes this separation, as well as a credible basis for interpreting scriptural accounts of the origin of evil.

What is the root of evil? Where, when and how did evil originate? The monotheistic religions attribute evil to Satan. However, beyond identifying initial acts of disobedience committed by the first man and woman under the influence of Satan, they are not able to explain convincingly the origin of Satan and evil and how they control the lives of human beings.

One of the key problems of theology has been the question of Satan's origin. Where did such an evil being come from? Did God create him? Did he coexist with God from the beginning?

God is only good, wanting only love and goodness for His creation. For this reason, with the exception of fallen humans, everything in the cosmos exists according to one, perfect order, reflecting the goodness of the Creator, God. Within a nature of pure goodness how can there be a base for creating an evil being? God would not have created Satan as an evil being because there is nothing evil within God. Furthermore, God's unceasing efforts to save His children from Satan and evil imply that human beings can indeed be saved. In other words, Satan's existence could not have preceded or paralleled the existence of God because Satan would then be eternal, and evil would be a part of human life forever. This would mean that salvation from evil would be impossible and God's work to save humankind a fruitless exercise. This leads to the conclusion that Satan was created as a good being but failed to fulfill his original, God-given purpose.

The Bible describes this being as a serpent, otherwise identified as the archangel Lucifer, while the Koran describes it as the jinn (or angel in some interpretations) Iblis. Whatever its exact identity, clearly it had a spiritual nature since, according to these scriptures, it understood God and God's word and was able to communicate with the first man and woman, Adam and Eve. In the Bible and Koran it is described as having a masculine nature and is said to have been created to serve Adam and Eve. In this text, therefore, the spiritual being known as Lucifer or Iblis will simply be called the Servant. As a servant of God and human beings, Lucifer/Iblis was part of God's creation, a good being. Once the Servant acted against the will of God, however, he became known as Satan.

Men and women were created to be inheritors of God's parental heart, to be like His children, while the other spiritual entities were to be His servants. Although servants have their own value in the creation, their relationship to God is not as intimate as that of His children. God loves all the creation but the capacity of children to receive the love of God is greater than that of servants. Therefore, the parent-child relationship between God and humans is more profound than the master-servant relationship between God and the Servant. Furthermore, a servant must be humble to the parents and the children of the family he serves, always respecting and deferring to the special intimacy of the parent-child relationship.

Knowledge is an essential element of spiritual nature and to know is to be responsible. To take responsibility for what one knows, a person must have the power of choice, which is intrinsic to free will. Adam, Eve and the Servant had to choose between obedience and disobedience to the commandment of God, which, according to scriptural accounts, prohibited them from eating the fruit of a particular tree. While the Judeo-Christian and Islamic scriptures leave ample room for diverse interpretations of what actually took place among these three key players in the world of God's original creation, they agree that Adam, Eve and the Servant all committed acts of disobedience. But what did God's prohibition really mean and what was the nature of their disobedience? What could motivate disobedience in these pure creations of God, when, according to God's warnings, they had everything (including their spiritual lives) to lose by disobedience and everything to gain through obedience?

The Mission of Adam, Eve and the Servant

Adam and Eve were created by God to fulfill the purpose of human beings by realizing the three blessings. They were to grow through three stages to perfect their giving and receiving of love, first as a true son and daughter, then as a true brother and sister. Once mature as individuals they would become husband and wife and, finally, father and mother. As true parents they would give birth to true children whom they would raise according to God's will within the realm of His true love. Their family would be the starting point of a true clan, tribe, nation and world, and its mature members and descendants would be kings and queens in human society and lords of love over the rest of creation.

Adam and Eve were to inherit from God true love, life and lineage, and, through incarnating the image of God in creation, become the ancestors of true love, life and lineage for all humankind. Their lives were to be models of individual responsibility and maturity, and of harmonious existence with other people and nature. Their family was to embody the ideal of true love, actualizing a standard of loving relationships that would last forever as an example for all humankind.

But who was there to guide Adam and Eve to fulfill their mission? Without substantial parents to educate them during the period of their growth, how could they be expected to accomplish their predestined purpose? God was their invisible, spiritual parent, but Adam and Eve were created as immature children who lacked the character needed to understand God directly. Since

God did not have true parents to use in educating Adam and Eve, He assigned the Servant to raise Adam and Eve. The Servant's mission was to guide them in their growth and the fulfillment of their purpose. Thus the Servant was given a position of great responsibility caring for Adam and Eve.

The Fall of Adam and Eve

But something went drastically wrong. Instead of educating them about God's love and truth and their purpose in life, the Servant led them into rebellion against God, causing them to lose their purity and their relationship with their spiritual parent. In the darkness of their separation from God, they created a family of self-centered love that was ignorant of God and became the dwelling of Satan. And instead of establishing a tradition of true love, life and lineage that could be passed from generation to generation, Adam and Eve created a legacy of satanic love, life and lineage: a world of Hell instead of Heaven.

Inheriting the perversion of his parents, Cain, their first son, killed his younger brother, Abel, in a fit of anger, revealing the depravity of his lineage and sealing the dismal fate of his family and its descendants. Thus Adam and Eve fell spiritually from a position of great importance as the children of God to become children of Satan who created a Hell of false love in which men and women lived in ignorance of the love and truth of God.

The Motive and Process of the Fall

What force could have enticed Adam and Eve to disobey God? Since they were warned of the dire consequences of disobedience, there must have been a powerful temptation for them to do the very thing that God had forbidden them. That Adam and Eve succumbed to the desire to eat a literal fruit is not credible, given the abundance of natural foods available for their sustenance. Furthermore, they were warned that they would die if they "ate the fruit," a risk even a starving person would be most unlikely to take. After eating the forbidden fruit they continued to live for a long time, implying that the fruit they ate was not literal but represented something of deep significance to their spiritual lives. What's more, when confronted by God after the fall, Adam and Eve covered their sexual parts, suggesting guilt associated with love rather than the consumption of food (in which case it would have made more sense for them to cover their mouths in shame).

According to the Principle, the only force greater than truth, and therefore capable of leading humans to disobey the laws of God, is love. God's essence is Heart and the very reason He created was to express the love of His Heart. Human purpose is fulfilled when individuals reciprocate God's love, giving joy to the Creator and His creation. Therefore, nothing can be superior to love in the creation. God's laws exist to guide humankind in the perfection of love: they exist to serve love. If it were otherwise, God's intention for the creation could not be fulfilled. Thus the only force powerful enough to tempt Adam and Eve into disobeying God's commandment was love. The force of the Principle was not as powerful as the force of love, but the force of the Principle combined with the force of God's commandment was stronger than the force of love. Therefore, as long as Adam and Eve obeyed the commandment they were strong enough to overcome the temptation to misuse love.

The object of growth is the perfection of love. Thus the most important task of the Servant was to teach Adam and Eve how to love according to God's will. But the Servant did not do as he was instructed by God.

A scenario of what took place in the fall, seen through the eyes of the Principle and corroborated by prevalent patterns of sinful behavior evident throughout history and the contemporary world, pictures the following unfolding of events.

As Adam and Eve approached maturity, they developed their capacity to give and receive true love, in the process embodying the beauty of their Creator more and more. This development of their spiritual natures meant they were growing in their ability to know and communicate with God directly, thus reducing their need for the Servant as God's parental representative.

The Servant sensed that his parental role was to end and that he was to take up his permanent position as a servant of Adam and

Eve. This change in his relationship with Adam and Eve did not change God's love for the Servant, but, given the wrong interpretation, it did create an opportunity for the Servant to feel he was losing God's love. From God's viewpoint, the Servant would completely fulfill his purpose, and become a greater object of love, by humbly serving Adam and Eve, but from the Servant's point of view he was confronted with a loss of position and love.

Furthermore, the Servant had to face the truth that he was not to participate in the three blessings of Adam and Eve and that they were going to receive God's love in a special way open only to human beings. Their beauty and potential to give and receive love was a cause of jealousy to the Servant, even though he was made by God to be fulfilled according to his own characteristics and potentialities. The Servant was unable to accept that his special role as God's representative to Adam and Eve was only for a limited time and that his permanent role and eternal value were as a beloved servant rather than a beloved son.

There were two possible responses the Servant could make to this development. He could share God's increasing delight in the growth of His children, or he could feel jealous of God's parental affection for Adam and Eve and seek to replace the love from God he felt he was losing. Unfortunately he chose the second course by pursuing a relationship of love with Eve. He sought her love to benefit himself rather than caring for Adam and Eve and seeing that they got what they needed to reach maturity and fulfill the three blessings. The masculine nature of the Servant inclined him towards Eve, whose femininity was particularly attractive to him. But in pursuing this relationship with Eve the Servant was leaving his position as a guardian of God's children and usurping the position of Adam, who was created to be the spouse of Eve.

When scriptures say the Servant encouraged Eve to eat of the fruit, in fact he encouraged Eve to share her love with him, disobeying God's instruction to the contrary. There were no literal fruits created by God that were not for human beings to enjoy because all fruits were to be taken in their season and for their proper purpose. Eve's mature love was to be given fully to Adam once she had reached womanhood and was qualified to be a true wife to him. Any other use of her womanly love was contrary to God's will.

Eve was attracted to the Servant because of his superior knowledge, and her good sisterly heart reached out to comfort him in his
'loss'. But by responding to the Servant's unrighteous love (by
agreeing to 'eat the fruit'), Eve lost her purity and her natural ability to give and receive true love. She learned perverted love from
her teacher, losing her position as God's true daughter and her
qualification to be a true wife and mother. Although the Servant
was only a spiritual being and Eve was a human being living on
earth, the love they consummated was sexual and substantial to
the point of violating the laws of true love. (The fact of substantial
sexual relations between spirits and people on earth is well docu-
mented in the literature on incubi — male spirits — and succubi
—female spirits — who engage in intercourse with members of the
opposite sex.) God could not accept or participate in the relationship between the Servant and Eve because it had nothing to do
with His standard of love. The unprincipled love relationship between them caused a spiritual fall, in which the two participants
cut themselves off from the true love of God. (The fall in this text
means loss of unity with God. It does not have any literal position-
al connotation.)

From her fallen position Eve could no longer understand God
and His will for her. But she could see that Adam was good and,
feeling ashamed of her disobedience, she could clearly understand
that she had been deceived by the Servant into having an illicit relationship with him. She realized that she should have waited to be
blessed in marriage with Adam, once they had reached maturity.
Eve was faced with a choice. She could repent of her error and con-
fess her sin to Adam, thereby separating herself from the Servant
and his false love, and allow Adam to help her restore her relationship with God. Or she could incriminate Adam in her mistake and
try to lose her sense of loss and isolation from God by drawing him
into a relationship of love with her by getting him to 'eat the fruit'
as well. She chose the second course of action, and Adam, even
though he knew it was clearly against God's commandment, abandoned his purity and entered into a relationship of premature conjugal love with her, premature because he had not yet reached full
mind–body unity (the first blessing), which was a precondition for
blessing in marriage, and because Eve, unrestored after the fall, was

not yet qualified to be his spouse. God could not recognize or participate in their love relationship because it violated the principles of true love. The ideal world of the three blessings could never be fulfilled through the practice of immature love. The premature sexual relationship between Adam and Eve is called the physical fall.

Eve's seduction of Adam did not liberate her from the misery she had fallen into, it merely drew Adam down to the same fallen realm. Through the fall, both Adam and Eve lost previously close relationships with God and were cut off from His true love. Now distant from God's heart and love, they created a distorted imitation of true man-woman love, patterned after Eve's relationship with the Servant. Thus instead of receiving God's blessing in marriage and creating a true love family, Adam and Eve established a fallen standard of love in a family that was blocked from receiving the love of God. Their impure love became the standard inherited by their children and subsequent generations of humankind.

Each had reason to blame the other for their fall. Adam blamed Eve for having deceived him into a premature love relationship, and Eve blamed Adam for not protecting her from the wiles of the Servant and for responding to her affections when he should have known that they were not sanctioned by God. By harboring these resentments for each other instead of repenting and asking God's and each other's forgiveness, Adam and Eve created a home of acrimony and bitterness, a loveless environment that was a dwelling for Satan rather than God. Raised in that satanic home, the children of Adam and Eve never received the parental love they needed to grow into true men and women. Instead they inherited the patterns of unprincipled interaction that turned the Garden of Eden into Hell on earth.

Evidence the Fall was a Misuse of Love

Both religion and science confirm that the misuse of love in the family is the root cause of evil and human suffering. Religion teaches that men and women must be responsible in the creation of families, and stipulates the harshest punishments for those who break God's commandments regarding these matters. In particular, adultery and other forms of illicit love are strictly forbidden and, in many traditions, punishable by death.

The social sciences confirm that the family is the key to the creation of a healthy society (or its opposite). The breakdown of man–woman love results in a breakdown of the family unit, producing all societal problems, from alcohol and drug abuse to juvenile delinquency and crime. Of particular concern to psychologists and sociologists is the rise of child abuse in families with immature, unloving parents. Moral decline has been the terminal sickness of all civilizations which have passed into history. The rapid decline of morality in secularized societies today has produced a plethora of sociological problems, ranging from those of single-parent families and abused children to the growing ranks of the homeless and soaring rates of debilitating addictions.

Medical scientists and practitioners add their own corroboration of the damage caused by family breakdown through the evidence they have gathered of the harm inflicted on society by venereal diseases, which are spread primarily through illicit love relationships. In particular, the AIDS epidemic, which is the direct consequence of widespread contemporary immorality, threatens the lives of a growing percentage of humankind.

Since the family is the basis for creation of a healthy (or sick) society and world, only when true love is restored to man–woman and parent–child relalionships can there be a permanent solution to the many problems that afflict human relations, from familial disunity and social disorder to racial conflicts and international wars.

Conclusion

The purpose of God's creation was shattered by the misuse of love, the most powerful force in the universe. The first man and woman never completed their growth to maturity and failed to create a true, Godly family and a loving dominion over nature. Instead they put their own wishes above those of God, in the process destroying the very means by which they could have fulfilled their deepest desires. Since the unprincipled love relationship between Eve and the Servant took place on the spiritual level, while the premature sexual relationship between Adam and Eve was both spiritual and physical, the fall of Adam and Eve occurred in two stages. When their son, Cain, killed his brother, Abel, the fall of Adam's family was completed and humanity embarked upon a history of misery and suffering, cut off from a relationship with God and the true love, life and lineage that come from Him alone.

The results of the fall were catastrophic, plunging humankind into a spiritual darkness so profound that thousands of years have passed without a solution being found to human separation from God. Without the Creator's parental love and goodness planted in the hearts of His beloved children, the original value of life was lost and, consequently, human beings have known only distortions and perversions of God's ideal. Some of the most serious repercussions of the fall are discussed in the following chapter.

8 | RESULTS OF THE FALL

INTRODUCTION

Adam and Eve began life as a couple on a foundation of mutual resentment and accusation, with each blaming the other for the predicament into which they had fallen instead of taking responsibility for their own role in the disaster. Having lost their original, intimate relationship with God, they lacked the heart and love to help each other out of the situation. And with the Servant having become Satan, the unrepentant master of false love instead of a wise teacher, there was no one to show them the way back to God.

The promise of the creation was shattered by the fall, and the very fabric of human relationships based on true love, out of which the ideal world was to have been made, was torn asunder. This left only incomplete and inadequate love relationships as the foundation for human society. The result was the creation of a world ignorant of God, populated by people pursuing purposes far removed from God's purpose for them. In their ignorance, fallen men and women have struggled against each other to gain a dominion of self-centered power over other people and the world of nature. Their pursuit of unrighteous desire for selfish purposes has made the world a place of conflicts and misery instead of an environment of love and peace.

The Loss of True Love

Adam and Eve's experience of love was colored by the fall: they had never received the true love of parents because the Servant had used the parental position given him by God to his own advantage; they had not achieved true brotherly-sisterly love (as evidenced by Adam's neglect of his sister when she entered a relationship of great jeopardy with the Servant) because the Servant had sought Eve for himself rather than educating Adam and Eve about their proper roles and relationship; and their experience of conjugal love had been completely invaded by Satan as it was based on the unprincipled relationship between the Servant and Eve. Even though they felt shame and remorse for their error, and God felt parental sympathy for His fallen children, God had to abide strictly by the Principle in leading them back to their original, pure positions.

The Servant had interfered in the love relationships of Adam and Eve because he was envious of the love they were receiving from God and jealous of the love they would consummate once they received God's blessing in marriage. He sought the experience of conjugal love for himself, usurping the place of Adam as Eve's spouse. The Servant became Satan when he acted on his unrighteous desire for Eve by seducing her instead of seeking the guidance of God in solving the confusion of his heart brought about by the change in his relationship with Adam and Eve: becoming their servant after being like their parent.

The Servant's invasion and destruction of the true love relationships of Adam and Eve made him, as Satan, the great enemy of pure love and of humankind's fulfillment of the second blessing. The universal experience of fallen people is frustration caused by their inability to experience the true love that every human being wants and seeks in life. The love relationships between parents and children, brothers and sisters, husbands and wives have always fallen short of the ideal. This is because the patterns of human love are based on those established by the first man and woman. Imperfect love has been passed from generation to generation: children raised with inadequate love are unable to perfect their own love and consequently are not qualified to give true love to their children. Human love has been associated with fear and guilt instead of fulfillment and joy.

The only way this cycle of imperfect love can be broken is through the creation of a new lineage, free from Satan's domination. A true man and woman must create a true family founded on relationships of true love. This family will then be the beginning point of a new, pure lineage that will fulfill the original ideal of God's creation. The central goal of history after the fall of Adam and Eve was precisely that: the restoration of fallen man and woman to the purity of Adam and Eve before the fall, through the mission of true parents. The true parents have to restore the true love, life and lineage that were lost in the fall.

The Loss of Truth

Adam and Eve lived in confusion, aware that they had made mistakes but unable to free themselves of the consequences. With their spiritual senses darkened, the God they had been growing to know and love was suddenly invisible to them. He was hidden from view behind the haze of their unprincipled lives which were dominated by the fallen love learned from the Servant. With this love God would have no relationship.

Their loss of God's love was accompanied by a loss of God's truth. In place of a clear, God-centered understanding of their purpose and how they were to fulfill it, they were fundamentally ignorant of their reason for being, of how to live a good life, create a good family and establish true dominion over nature. Thus the home of Adam and Eve became Satan's home and not God's home, an environment of false love and ignorance instead of a dwelling place for God's love and truth. Their children were brought up knowing only Satan's standard of distorted love as well as the partial truths and outright falsehoods that Satan had imparted to their parents. Coming from this unprincipled home environment, Cain was raised with satanic tendencies which eventually led him to repeat the sin of Satan by murdering Abel: Adam and Eve had been killed spiritually by Satan, who destroyed their relationship with God. The ignorance of Adam and Eve was inherited by their children.

The ignorance of Adam and Eve was the result of their inversion of the mind–body relationship. A true man or woman grows to maturity by the mind maintaining the subject position over the body.

God communicates His will to the mind of human beings, so the body must obey the mind if an individual is to become the image of God. When the interests of the body are placed above those of the mind the basic order of creation is violated and chaos results. This is rather like a rider putting his horse in charge of following directions on a map to reach a hidden treasure. The result will not be a success: horses are made to follow humans, not to lead them. Led by the instincts of his body, a human being is totally lost in this world, stumbling through life until he arrives at the end of his physical existence when, on beginning life in the spirit world, he is confronted with the consequence of his ignorance: an existence in darkness and confusion far from the light and truth of God.

Good and Evil

The fundamental ignorance of Adam and Eve after the fall was their inability to distinguish between good and evil. They could not clearly recognize how their lives contradicted God's will. Any thought or deed that contributes to the fulfillment of human purpose, the achievement of the three blessings, is good. Conversely, any thought or action that stands in the way of human fulfillment is evil. Put in a different way, any base people make for God to work is good whereas any base for Satan to work is evil.

Things in themselves are not intrinsically good or evil. The way they are employed (for or against God's will) determines their value. For example, a hammer used to build a family home is 'good', whereas the same hammer is 'evil' if used as a murder weapon. By the same token, a gun used in the defense of a nation against unrighteous attack is 'good', but used to kill an innocent person is 'evil'. Hammer and gun are not good or evil in themselves, but their use by people is.

Thus the Principle does not agree with classical dualism which places good and evil in the same category as night and day, black and white, man and woman. Good and evil are not complementary dual characteristics of God and His creation, rather good is the result of God-centered activity and evil the result of any activity contrary to the will of God. Since God is only good, everything He created has the original nature to do good. Evil results when created beings do not act according to the purpose for which they were created. Thus good and evil are contradictory opposites that can have nothing to do with each other, whereas dual characteristics are complementary aspects of creation that are essential to its existence, activity and multiplication. There is no evil in God's ideal world.

Satan was able to maintain his influence over Adam and Eve because they obeyed him instead of God, and thus voluntarily established a base within themselves that remained responsive to him. They could not clearly identify this base since they had lost the purity with which to judge the impurity of Satan's influence. Thus Adam and Eve fell under an evil influence that they could not understand.

This has been Satan's hold on the descendants of Adam and Eve. They have experienced the resentments and lusts of Satan without knowing the origin of those feelings and without the purity to clearly identify them as foreign to their true, original natures. Satan has been like a criminal kingpin who walks freely in society, unrecognized and unprosecuted because his crimes remain unknown.

The efforts of fallen men and women to do good are conditioned by the evil they have inherited from their ancestors, all the way back to Adam and Eve. Thus the standard of goodness of fallen humans is relative. Only the standard of goodness of a sinless person, completely free of Satan's influence, is absolute. The true parents, who are to replace Adam and Eve as ancestors of a sinless lineage, set the standard of absolute goodness as a model for all people to emulate. Without such a model, fallen humans cannot identify the criminal Satan and separate themselves completely from him.

The original nature of man and woman is the image of God. This can never be completely lost, but it is smothered by fallen impulses and characteristics that became a dominant part of human nature as a result of the fall. This fallen, evil nature inclines people to follow directions opposite to their original direction and true purpose. There is a continuous struggle between the evil mind and the original mind of fallen humans. These internal conflicts are the cause of conflicts between individuals and families, tribes and nations. The original nature of human beings, on the other hand, inclines them towards uniting in harmony around a common, God-centered purpose.

It is never the original nature of man or woman that guides them into relationships of illicit love or inspires aggression and violence against others. Neither does it lead a man to hate his own brother or sister, or condemn a husband and wife to share a life of resentment and bitterness. It does not incite children to rebel against their parents, nor does it cause parents to neglect and abuse their children. Neither is it original nature that causes humans to abuse the rest of creation. The evil mind of fallen people produces all human wrongdoing and causes all human suffering by leading individuals to disobey God.

The Influence of Good and Evil Spirits

The struggle between original mind and evil mind is greatly exacerbated by the intervention of spirit men and women in the affairs of people on earth. As explained in Chapter 5, spirits that have not reached maturity must serve their descendants and good people on earth in order to gain the benefit of vitality elements. Good spirits, that is those close to God, have a beneficial influence on the spirits of men and women on earth. However, evil spirits, who are distant from God because of their lack of development, are close to Satan in character and direction and have a satanic influence on the spirits of people on earth. Because of the dislocation of spirit and body brought about by the fall, fallen individuals are generally unaware of the influence of good and evil spirits in their lives. They tend to attribute fallen spiritual influences to their own moods, sentiments and inspirations.

Whenever the spirit of a fallen man or woman unites with the thoughts or activities of evil spirits he or she multiplies the power of Satan and the evil in the world. Satan's power will only end when people cease interaction with his ideas and activities. In a world of relative good, this cannot be achieved altogether by fallen individuals. Only through a relationship with true parents, who are separated from Satan and manifest an absolute standard of goodness, can fallen people finally rid himself of all Satan's influences.

Fallen Nature

Careful analysis of the fallen nature of humankind reveals that it has four major components that derive from four fundamental errors at the time of the fall:

First, fallen humans fail to see people and situations as God sees them. Because of disbelief and distrust, they do not appreciate the value of their circumstances and those of others, leading to erroneous concepts and actions. All human sins (thoughts and actions which separate human beings from God) are the result of individuals taking positions contrary to God's point of view. This tendency is inherited from the Servant's failure to see Adam and Eve as God saw them. While God loved Adam and Eve as His children and wanted them to grow to fulfill the three blessings, the Servant came to want a relationship with them for his own benefit. The Servant was willing to sacrifice Adam and Eve for his own pleasure. This self-centered rather than God-centered point of view led the Servant to act in error, destroying God's ideal. The Servant's disbelief and distrust of God led to his outright rebellion against God, and was passed on to Adam and Eve and their descendants as the most fundamental aspect of fallen nature.

Second, lacking God's perspective, fallen people have a tendency to misjudge their own value, to be arrogant and to go their own way in seeking power and prestige at the cost of the fulfillment of God's will. They are not satisfied with what they have and seek to gain for themselves what belongs to others. This fallen nature comes from the Servant's dissatisfaction with his position as the teacher and servant of Adam and Eve. Failing to recognize his own value and special role in the creation, the Servant aspired to stand above his God-given position and thirsted for the position of Adam as the first son of God and spouse of Eve, a role specifically forbidden to him. This type of arrogance blocks the human path to God, and is the root of adultery.

Third, as a result of the second fallen nature, human beings tend to dominate those they should follow. This reversal of dominion causes chaos in human relations. For example, the prophets and saints sent by God typically have been rejected and persecuted by the very people they tried to assist, bringing disaster to those people. This aspect of fallen nature is inherited from the Servant who inverted the natural order of God's creation by claiming a position over Adam and Eve. Adam was to have been in the subject position to Eve, and both of them were to have been subject over the Servant. In effect, God was excluded from His rightful position as Adam and Eve's parent and lord because they put the Servant in God's position. Because Adam and Eve elevated Satan to God's position, in the fallen world Satan exerts an unrighteous dominion over God's people, a dominion established over the first family and continued to the present.

Fourth, fallen humans tend to seek others to share in their wrongdoing rather than taking responsibility to correct it themselves. They justify their evil deeds and try to win approval and participation from others. This multiplication of evil is responsible for the fallen culture in which widespread complicity in unprincipled behavior prevents its eradication. This nature comes from Eve who wanted to rid herself of the guilt and shame she felt after her relationship with the Servant, but instead of repenting repeated an unprincipled act of love with Adam, thus multiplying evil instead of reversing it. In fallen society it is common for people to want to minimize their sense of guilt by including others in what they know to be wrongdoing. This behavior is precisely the opposite of taking responsibility. Irresponsible action causes the multiplication of evil.

The four aspects of fallen nature became deeply rooted in the first family, and from it they were passed down to subsequent generations as inherited fallen nature. The reality of this inheritance was made fully evident by the behavior of Cain, the first child of Adam and Eve: he failed to share God's love for Abel; he sought to dominate his younger brother; he cut God off from Abel and his lineage by killing him; and he multiplied evil by committing murder in imitation of Satan's spiritual murder of Adam and Eve.

Human beings must rid themselves of all four aspects of fallen nature if they are to become free to unite with God. As the root of the human tree, the behavior of Adam and Eve affected all their descendants. The tree itself is intrinsically good, but it is suffering from an ailment that has spread from the root to the leaves. The fallen nature is something that all men and women inherit, and it affects their lives, whether they are aware of it or not. To identify clearly the four aspects of fallen nature within him, an individual must check himself against the absolute standard of true parents.

Why God did not Prevent the Fall

Considering the world of evils that sprang from the fallen lineage of Adam and Eve, one might well wonder why God did not intervene to prevent the fall. The answer lies in human responsibility. Since Adam, Eve and the Servant all had free will, they were free to obey or disobey God. They had been created by God with free will because He wanted them to love Him out of their own volition. There is no love other than that given freely.

If God had intervened to prevent Adam and Eve from falling when He saw them deviating from their true path He would have violated His own principles, which require human beings to fulfill their own portion of responsibility in order to grow to maturity. The implication would have been that God had erred when he made Adam and Eve, and that He then had to act to fix the mistake. But God had not made a mistake. Adam and Eve had to have free will to fulfill their purpose. Only through exercising their free will with responsibility could Adam and Eve fulfill their purpose for existence.

In sum, then, God did not prevent the fall because: He had not made a mistake in creating human beings with free will; because humans must fulfill their own portion of responsibility; and because love, for which human beings were created, can only be given out of human free will.

Why Humankind Needs True Parents

The fall of Adam and Eve meant the postponement of God's will until such time as a new Adam and new Eve could take their place and fulfill the three blessings. It also meant that fulfilling humanity's original purpose became nothing more than a hope for fallen people, a promised Kingdom of Heaven instead of a reality from the beginning of human existence.

In the fallen world, Satan and satanic ideas, relationships and institutions prevail, and every initiative from God's side has to fight against the tide of fallen humanity. Children are born with contradictory natures that are both inclined to goodness and burdened by the legacy of fallen behavior inherited from their ancestors. This legacy tempts them to violate God's laws and makes them susceptible to the false love that dominates the fallen world.

God has sent special persons and groups to teach and enlighten confused people in the fallen realm. The history of religion is the history of these representatives of God and the efforts they have made to challenge the fallen status quo with God's love and truth. They have always been met with hostility and suffered persecution because Satan's dominion is most threatened by men and women who devote their lives to God and the service of humankind.

The struggle for God begins within the individual. Unless the mind gains dominion over the body, the original nature over the fallen nature, one cannot succeed in subjugating the evil of the outside world. This has been understood, practiced and taught by all the great figures in God's providence, from Noah to Mohammed, as well as the saints of modern times.

As long as people are born into the fallen lineage of Adam and Eve, their fallen natures limit them from completely separating from Satan and becoming one with God. Thus the whole object of human history, seen from God's viewpoint, has been to restore Adam and Eve and create a new first family so that a new, pure lineage can be established in the midst of the fallen world. This new lineage will eventually supplant the lineage dominated by Satan. A new Adam and Eve will be true parents who restore love, life and lineage to God's dominion and who thereby create the God-centered families, tribes, nations and world that God has always wanted and virtuous human nature has always yearned for.

The mission of true parents is that of Adam and Eve: the fulfillment of human purpose on earth through the accomplishment of the three blessings. The restoration of Adam alone (as the Judeo-Christian savior or messiah) is not sufficient. Only a couple, a sinless man and woman, can establish a purified lineage. The pervasive and dominant presence of evil in the world makes their task extremely difficult, but there is no other route to salvation.

Conclusion

The fall occurred when the Servant disunited with God and left his position as educator and guardian of Adam and Eve to seduce Eve. Adam and Eve established a family centered on Satan rather than God, creating a lineage that carried to their descendants all the evil elements of their disobedience. The force that caused them to violate God's laws was love misused to satisfy selfish purposes. The misuse of love has therefore remained the fundamental problem of human society.

To end the dominion of Satan and create a world of true love centered on God, true parents must come to restore fallen love, life and lineage to God. This purpose has been the central thrust of history. Part Three of this book, which follows, examines the principles and historical processes of restoring true parents for humankind.

PART
III

THE HISTORY OF
RESTORATION

INTRODUCTION

Looking back over the thousands of years of human history, it seems incredible that the failure of just one couple, Adam and Eve, at the beginning of human existence, could produce such a ghastly record of human imperfection and suffering, involving the lives of billions of people. For many who question God, it is this sad history and the profound problems of the world today that make belief so difficult. How can one believe in a good God if the world He made is so full of suffering and misery?

The answer lies in the nature of God's relationship with human beings. The principles that govern that relationship were made by God to bring joy to both Creator and creation. A central element of those principles is that humans exercise their free will responsibly, in accordance with God's will. When people are disobedient to God they violate God's principles and create chaos and suffering. Thus humankind's obedience or disobedience to God shapes human life and history.

History and the world present many baffling realities that beg explanation. Why, for example, has the history of evil been drawn out for so long? What has been accomplished for God in all the thousands of years since Adam and Eve, and what has yet to be accomplished? What roles did the various religious figures of the past play in God's plan to restore human beings to their original purity? How can evil be finally eliminated? If these and related questions cannot be answered conclusively by believers, their faith in God will not be well-grounded or convincing to others in a world under constant assault by secular systems.

For modern individuals to be powerful and focused in their lives of faith they need to comprehend God's thinking and activities in the world today, which can only be understood clearly in the context of His thinking and activities in history. It is not enough to have a general belief based on abstract faith. After all, many crimes have been committed and many wars fought by people professing faith in God and believing Him to be on their side, even though other believers, and even fellow-religionists, have been the victims of those crimes and the enemies in those wars.

God does not have a contradictory purpose; His unitary nature prevents Him from working against Himself. It is only the inadequacy of human understanding of God that produces disagreement, confusion and conflict among believers.

The situation in the world today was produced by a historical battle between forces of good and evil. God and Satan cannot coexist harmoniously because their purposes are opposite. Therefore, the struggle between good and evil will continue until Satan is finally defeated by the true love of God. How can a believer contribute to God's victory? How can he know what God wants of him in his life? To be close to God, to serve God in the most meaningful way, believers need to know where the battle's front line is and what God most wants them to do to help in the work of restoration. These things can only be known through an understanding of the historical processes that produced the situation in the world today.

The following chapters explain the principles that govern the process of restoration and describe the highpoints centered on the lives of central figures chosen by God to play pivotal roles in that history. This outline of providential history provides a framework for understanding the role played by major religions in God's overall restoration scheme and how the process of restoration affects today's world.

Because of the vastness and complexity of human history, this account is necessarily extremely limited, focusing only on some of the most important people and events in the long process of restoration. However, the history of restoration, which is the subject matter of scriptures, is the central history of humankind and other, secular histories are of secondary importance as being the result of internal developments. Since all humankind is to be restored, every people, race and nation has its own restoration history, usually centered around the rise of a religion. Through the fall, the position of true parents was lost and consequently God's providence has been focused on restoring one man and one woman to stand in that position as the beginning point of salvation for all humankind. Therefore it is those historical developments most directly related to the advent of true parents that will be discussed in the following chapters.

In making its emphasis the principles of restoration and their application in history, this text does not set out to reconcile itself with existing scriptural accounts of God's providence through exegesis. That is the purpose of other explanations of the Principle. Rather, it presents an account of God's work with His children in history that reveals His principles operating in human affairs. Thus readers will recognize many familiar figures and events from history in the following pages but find the contextual perspective offered here to be new. If there appear to be conflicts between traditional scriptural accounts, or interpretations of such accounts, and this one, the reader will be able to judge these contents on the merits of the overall integrity of the Principle.

9 | THE PRINCIPLES OF RESTORATION

INTRODUCTION

With the fall of Adam and Eve, God's intimate relationship with the children of His love was lost. As the Heavenly Father of humankind, He had to deal with sinful man and woman rather than innocent and pure beings capable of understanding His Heart and will. Although the parental love of God would always seek to embrace Adam and Eve and their descendants, there was no one with whom God could share His deep feelings of love and no one who could carry out His will for the creation of an ideal world. God's was the most lonely situation, like that of a parent whose children have been kidnapped and killed by a jealous and rebellious servant.

Since God's will is eternal and unchanging, His original purpose for creating humankind was not changed by the fall of Adam and Eve. However, for fallen men and women to fulfill that purpose became extremely difficult. Adam and Eve had lost the internal qualities needed to be children of God and lords over creation. As a result, life for them and for all humankind became very difficult, both spiritually and physically. Separated from God, people have not understood how to live a virtuous life and maintain themselves physically. In their spiritual ignorance, they have developed adversarial rather than harmonious relationships with their fellow humans and with nature. In the original world, natural human impulses were pure and guided people to God. In the fallen world, natural impulses are, more often than not, governed by fallen nature and, if obeyed, lead people to disaster.

As a parent of infinite heart, God would never allow His beloved children, however serious their mistakes, to be cast into the realm of Satan forever. On the contrary, each and every one has to be restored to his or her original nature and purpose. God restores fallen humanity using the same principles of creation by which He originally made humankind. Applied to the circumstances of fallen humans, the principles of creation become the *principles of recreation,* or restoration. This chapter explains how the *principles of restoration* operate in human lives and in history, both on earth and in the spirit world.

The Goal of Restoration History

The fundamental problem of fallen human beings is that they lack true parents to raise them with true love to fulfill their original purpose. Without true parents, inevitably they are dominated by Satan through the sinful lineage inherited from the first human ancestors. Thus the key to restoring fallen humans is establishing true parents in place of the false parents, Adam and Eve. Once true parents exist, a pure new lineage, transmitting true love and free from Satan's dominion, can develop as a model for the rest of the world and the point of entry for a complete return to God.

Because only true parents can create a world of God's dominion and end Satan's control of humankind, the history of restoration centers on restoring first one man, a second Adam, and then one woman, a second Eve. The true family they establish is the foundation for restoring clans, tribes, nations and, ultimately, the whole world. Thus history is not just a random sequence of events, it is a purposeful movement of humankind towards a goal: the restoration of fallen humanity, beginning with true parents.

Change of Lineage

Once the position of true parents is established and a new, purified lineage begun, the purification of all fallen humanity can begin. Ultimately, the restoration of fallen men and women is achieved through their *change of lineage* from Adam and Eve's fallen line to the sinless line of true parents. The most internal purpose of restoration history is, then, the change of fallen lineage, under Satan's dominion, to true lineage, under God's dominion. Although the scope of this text does not permit a complete explanation of the purification of lineage in preparation for the messiah and his bride, nor does it explain the process of engrafting by which fallen men and women are 'reborn' into the lineage of true parents, readers should know that the core objective of the restoration process, the salvation of fallen humanity, is the change of lineage.

The Principles of Restoration

To understand the process of restoration, one must understand the principles that govern it.

God is a God of principle, of law. He Himself exists according to divine principles, He created according to these principles and He works to restore fallen humanity using these same perfect principles. History seen from God's point of view is the history of restoration governed by the principles of restoration.

How do the principles of restoration work?

As explained in Part One, the principles of creation are the basis for the realization of an ideal world, centered on God. Adam, Eve and the Servant all acted in violation of these principles, creating a world of distorted love and unprincipled relationships. The most basic law of restoration is that humans can eliminate the results of the fall only by reversing the behavior that led to the fall. Since the fundamental error of Adam and Eve was their failure to obey the word of God and their surrender to His enemy, the key to restoring their failure lies in living a life of faith in obedience to God and the voluntary surrender to His representative.

Because human beings are endowed with a portion of responsibility, God could not forgive Adam and Eve for their sin unconditionally without violating His own principles. The same applies to the descendants of the first ancestors. To be forgiven, fallen people must first repent of their sinfullness and then demonstrate their sincere desire to return to God by making efforts to obey God's word and fulfill their true purpose. This reverses the pattern of disobedience established by Adam and Eve. These conditions, together with acts of surrender, are called indemnity conditions. Thus, the essence of the principles of restoration can be summarized as follows: restoration is accomplished by fallen humanity making indemnity conditions.

The suffering of humanity, and in particular the suffering of individuals, groups and nations chosen by God to pioneer restoration, has all been related to payment of indemnity for the liberation of humankind from the dominion of Satan.

There are three kinds of indemnity conditions:

1. **Conditions of equal value:** Each person is responsible for any wrong done to others. That wrong must be indemnified by a condition of equal value, paid either to the same person or to someone in a similar situation. If indemnity is not paid on earth, it has to be paid in the spirit world, where the lack of a body makes payment of indemnity a great deal more difficult.

2. **Conditions of greater value:** When a person fails to make a condition, he has to restore not only that condition but also the failure as well. Thus the new condition has to be of greater value than the original condition. For example, when Abraham made a mistake in a sacrifice of animals he was called upon by God to offer his son as a sacrifice. The accumulation of unfulfilled conditions over time has made the restoration process incredibly complicated. People chosen to play key roles in the providence of restoration have to make indemnity conditions not only for their own restoration but also for the restoration of their ancestors, families, tribes, nations and even the whole of humankind, depending on their mission. Prophets and saints sent to liberate fallen humanity from the dominion of Satan have to make indemnity conditions on behalf of the people they want to help. The man and woman chosen to be true parents in place of Adam and Eve have to pay indemnity for all humanity.

3. **Conditions of lesser value:** Human beings cannot pay back the full value of what they lost in the fall and in subsequent generations of fallen existence. However, they must make conditional offerings of less value to demonstrate the sincerity of their desire to return to God. Given in a true spirit of faith, these offerings are accepted by God as conditions for forgiving the human debt of sin. In the restoration process, conditions of lesser value are paid by followers who benefit from the indemnity paid for them by their central figures who represent God. The followers of a prophet, for example, inherit his foundation of indemnity by demonstrating faith in him and living according to his instructions. Following in his footsteps is less difficult than pioneering the path. Ultimately, the universal conditions laid by the first couple to establish the position of true parents provide a foundation for all people who have faith in them to become true parents themselves, even though the conditions they have to make are less demanding than those made by the first true parents. The principle of making conditions of lesser value to achieve restoration is the basis of hope for fallen humans, who can never pay the full cost of restoration.

The Foundation for True Parents

The making of indemnity conditions is not an arbitrary process. Indemnity has to be paid with a clear purpose and according to an exact formula. There are two main objectives, the historical and the personal. The historical objective is to set up a foundation for the restoration of true parents. The personal objective is to set up an individual foundation to receive true parents and be spiritually 'grafted' to their lineage.

There are two stages in laying a *foundation for true parents*. The first, called the *foundation of faith*, is to restore the first thing Adam and Eve lost: their faith in the word of God (the commandment not to eat the fruit). The second condition, the *foundation of substance*, is to remove the result of Adam and Eve's disobedience: the corruption of their original, sinless nature into sinful fallen nature.

The Foundation of Faith

The first step fallen humans must take on the road back to God is to demonstrate faith in the word of God. Faith is demonstrated by making an offering to God, sacrificing what humans treasure for the sake of God. This reverses the mistake of Adam and Eve who chose self-gratification over obedience to God. Prayer, fasting and serving others are examples of such conditional offerings which indemnify Adam and Eve's disobedience and contribute to making a foundation of faith.

Since Adam and Eve brought destruction upon humankind by pursuing their own desires against the will of God, restoration of fallen nature ultimately requires the complete submission of human desires to the will of God. While this total surrender to God is the final stage of offering, the process begins with individuals offering their possessions and then, eventually, themselves. All men and women of God have had to go this way of suffering in order to attain spiritual maturity.

It is not enough merely to express an attitude of obedience to God's word. Because Adam's faith and obedience were to be upheld throughout the entire course of his growth to maturity, to restore the faith he lost requires a commitment of faith for a meaningful period of time. And because the central objective of restoration is fulfilling the three blessings, based on completion of the four position foundation, the time periods required for the creation of a foundation of faith typically relate to four positions reaching maturity through three stages of growth. The key providential numbers are 4, 12, 21 and 40.

Because of the importance of these numbers, in the separation of humans from Satan and the formation of a foundation of faith, they appear frequently in sacred history. For example, in the Bible and Koran the numbers 4, 12, 21 and 40 are common: Noah's faith was vindicated through 40 days of rain that led to 40 days of flooding; Jacob spent 21 years suffering under his uncle Laban in

Haran before returning to Canaan as a victor in faith; three times in his life Moses was called upon by God to demonstrate faith for 40-year periods (in Egypt, Midian and Sinai) and he had to build faith among the Israelites with 12 tribal leaders; Jesus fasted 40 days and ministered to his 12 disciples for 40 days after his resurrection; Mohammed began his public mission at age 40 and completed a victorious 21-year course before his death.

The Foundation of Substance

A person who demonstrates his desire to return to God by successfully establishing a foundation of faith is then able to take a substantial step of purification by laying a foundation of substance. The original, pure human nature was corrupted through the influence of Satan, who, as the Servant, sought the position that belonged to Adam and drew Eve into an unprincipled love relationship. When Eve submitted she abandoned her position as a daughter of God and bride of Adam and became a representative of Satan and his unprincipled love. Under the dominion of Satan, Adam and Eve inherited his unprincipled attitudes: self-centeredness, disobedience, resentment, arrogance and unrighteous lust for power, all derived from denying God's viewpoint. Instead of transmitting true love, life and lineage from God to their descendants, Adam and Eve became transmitters and multipliers of Satan's fallen love, life and lineage.

This means that all humanity, although endowed by God with an original nature that is free from sin, has inherited the nature of Satan. This fallen nature, with its tendency to evil, is at war with the original nature, which seeks only God and goodness. Within every fallen man and woman there is an original nature thirsting for liberation from Satan and oneness with God.

To break the dominion of Satan and remove his negative traits from their own natures, fallen men and women have to go through a process of restoring their relationships with God by subjugating Satan. As Adams and Eves they have to establish proper relations with Servants. The first step is for Adam to regain the position of subject over the Servant, who must surrender willingly as Adam's object. This is the key to restoring the original spiritual order and God's dominion over creation (1. God, 2. Adam, 3. Eve and 4. the Servant).

Adam lost his position through indulging in false love. The way to win back his position is through the practice of true love. An Adam figure must give God's love to a Servant figure so that the Servant can be won over to God's viewpoint and from his own volition accept Adam as his subject. The first man qualified to achieve this restoration totally is the restored Adam, or messiah.

When an Adam figure gives true love to a Servant figure, his own original nature gains ascendancy over his fallen nature, which would have him act in a selfish, satanic manner. Likewise, when the Servant accepts the love of Adam and becomes obedient to Adam, his original nature as a beloved and obedient servant of God gains ascendancy over his fallen nature as a disobedient and rebellious servant. Thus the purification of fallen humans, in which the good original nature becomes subject over the evil fallen nature, is accomplished through the restoration of good and proper relationships between Adam and the Servant. Once one man has been fully restored as a second Adam (the messiah) a woman can be restored as a second Eve. Restored Adam and Eve are true parents.

This restoration process applies to all fallen humanity. All people are put in positions that offer the opportunity to restore the fallen nature they inherited by restoring Adam-Servant type relationships. The key figures in the history of restoration have had to pioneer this path, both to lay foundations of faith and substance for the appearance of a second Adam and Eve, and to help others participate in that foundation-laying process so that all men and women can regain true love, life and lineage through their relationship with true parents. Since Adam is the first to be restored, the history of restoration features the central figures chosen by God to restore Adam. Once Adam and Eve have been restored, the Servant can be restored as well.

The foundation for true parents is laid by fallen humans through a process which enables them to achieve substantial purification of their fallen nature. Only a purified person can understand God's will and the dispensation for true parents, and therefore only a person who has been purified in this manner can be expected to unite with God's providence rather than oppose it.

True Human Love is Last to be Restored

The first thing to be lost, a true love relationship between man and woman, is the last thing to be restored. Complete purification of human love is the ultimate goal of history. True love exists where there is purity, and purification, or restoration, of fallen nature begins in the realm of the results of the fall, not the cause. Thus the path to restore the love between Adam and Eve begins with the restoration of the Servant-Adam relationship. The history of restoration reflects this in that providential figures were sent by God to establish foundations for true parents, who would bring true love, by laying foundations of faith and substance. As foundations for true parents were established in successive providential eras, the standard of man-woman love was raised. Thus in the era prior to God's first revelation of truth in the ten commandments, which included a prohibition against adultery, there was no established law for man–woman relations. When Jesus came on an even greater foundation than Moses, he said that to lust itself was an act of adultery. This high moral standard is to prepare fallen men and women to receive and then emulate the true love of true parents. Celibacy in Christianity (and other faiths) is a particular condition of purification for this purpose.

Once pure conjugal love is restored, a new lineage is founded and the complete salvation of fallen humanity can begin. The beginning of this pure lineage of true love marks the successful achievement of the goal of restoration, because through this lineage the dominion of Satan over humankind is broken and and a new history of goodness can begin.

The Role of Religion

The purpose of religion is to inspire and guide fallen man to establish foundations of faith and substance in preparation to receive true parents and become true parents themselves. Religious activity is not an end in itself, but only a means of purifying people. By demonstrating faith in God and then restoring relationships with others an individual creates the conditions necessary for restoration. The completion of this process, and therefore the ultimate objective of religion, is the creation of purified lineage, free from satanic influences. Once the necessary conditions have been laid, true parents can come and fulfill this purpose, opening the way for all other people to be engrafted into their restored lineage.

The continued fallen state of humankind, despite the great efforts made through the ages by countless prophets, sages and saints, proves that this restoration process has not been successfully completed. Religion has not yet accomplished its mission. Only when people do fulfill their responsibilities in obedience to God, as taught by religion, will the conditions for restoration be completed.

Religious history is the central, causal historical process because it has to do with God's uppermost concern for humanity: the restoration of Adam and Eve. Those individuals and groups that God chooses to lead the restoration providence are given primary responsibility to obey His laws and fulfill their missions. If they succeed, they are blessed as God's chosen ones, and through them others can be blessed as well. If they fail, however, they cause a delay in the providence for which they bear particular responsibility. All other historical developments are object to the history of restoration and should be examined in that context, however important they may seem on the surface.

Resurrection

Through the fall, human beings lost their intimate relationship with God. To be separated from God, the source of all love and life, is to die spiritually. Thus, in a spiritual sense, the Servant killed Adam and Eve when he invaded their love relationship.

Restoration of fallen human beings can be understood as resurrection of their dead spirits. Biblical and Koranic scriptures about resurrection are sometimes misunderstood to be referring to a physical phenomenon, but, according to the principle of creation, when a person dies his body has finished its purpose and disintegrates while his spirit continues to exist forever in the spirit world. It is fallen spirits and not dead bodies that need resurrection. What's more, taking on a new body would not bring an individual closer to God.

The Four Principles of Resurrection

The process of resurrection is accomplished according to the principles of creation applied to human beings in their fallen condition. Thus the principles of creation become principles of recreation, or resurrection. There are four principles of resurrection.

First, resurrection takes place through God's word, the truth. God created with His word and gave His word, the commandment, to Adam and Eve to guide them to completion. God has continued to give His word to fallen humans, to guide them back to their original purpose. The revelations of God's truth are the basis of religion. By obeying God's instructions, the fallen human spirit is separated from Satan and grows towards oneness with God in a step by step process of learning God's truth and applying what has been learned.

Second, resurrection takes place in three stages, formation, growth and completion. Through the fall, Adam and Eve descended spiritually from the top of the growth stage to a realm below even the formation stage. Thus the providence of restoration aims at raising fallen humans from below the formation stage to the top of the completion stage and into the direct dominion of God.

Third, because the human spirit needs vitality elements from the body in order to grow, resurrection takes place on the foundation of the physical body. This is true for people on earth and for the discarnate spirits of those who have died physically. As explained in Chapter 5, discarnate spirits tend to seek relations with people still on earth because they can grow spiritually by serving those who are doing good deeds for God and humanity.

The men and women called by God to accomplish important providential missions inevitably attract the support of good spirits who want to benefit by contributing to the providence as directly as possible. Good spirits can be very helpful in facilitating the missions of God's chosen people, but people on earth, with spirit and body united, must remain in the subject position over spirits since restoration takes place on earth.

Fourth, resurrection takes place according to the merits of the age. Only after a certain spiritual level has been opened up by a central figure of God can anyone else enter that level. Thus the great figures of restoration history, such as Confucius, Buddha, Moses, Jesus and Mohammed, pioneered new realms of resurrection for their followers to inherit.

In the history of restoration, each successful foundation laid on earth has opened up a new level of resurrection. The result on earth has been the development of enlightened cultures and civilizations, and in the spirit world of ever higher realms of being. The newly opened levels of resurrection are accessible to anyone who unites with the faith and deeds of the pioneers of those levels. The final stage of resurrection, the complete union of humans with God, will be accomplished by the true parents and then, through them, will become available to all other people. Complete resurrection is the destiny of all humankind since God's will for His creation can be fulfilled by no other means.

Returning Resurrection vs Reincarnation

Since spirits need to serve people on earth until they have reached full maturity of love, there is an active but invisible involvement of spirit men and women in the lives of people on earth. This is particularly the case at times of providential significance, when God, through a central figure, opens up a new level of resurrection. The central figure and his faithful followers on earth are the first to achieve the new realm, but spirits who assist them can also share in their resurrection. The return of spirits to earth to participate in the resurrection process is called *returning resurrection*. When it occurs, there are sometimes spiritual phenomena associated with it, such as people seeing visions, hearing voices or experiencing miraculous events in their lives.

However, the phenomena associated with returning resurrection are mistaken by some to be produced by spirits of immature people in the spirit world entering new-born bodies to fulfill their earthly responsibilities. This theory of reincarnation holds that the karma of individuals can only be paid off through this type of return to the physical world. But indemnity is paid by spirits through cooperation with good people on earth. For example, if a Christian leader were to experience the presence and assistance of the apostle Paul, it would mean that Paul was working with that leader for the sake of God's providence and for his own resurrection, and not that he had a new life on earth in the body of that leader. Each person is born with a spirit of his or her own, and any attempt by a discarnate spirit to enter the body of a new human being can only lead to spiritual possession.

Spiritual Influences in Human Life

The need of spirits to descend to earth to participate in resurrection also produces a wide range of spiritual phenomena that are not in themselves directly relevant to resurrection. Many types of mental illness are the result of spiritual interference in the lives of people who lack strong mind–body unity. Failure to put words into action makes a base for foreign spirits to interfere in a person's life, seeking to influence his thoughts and actions. A person may be troubled by a possessive relative or friend who has entered the spiritual world ahead of him, or by other spirits who simply want to use him for their own purposes. Only low spirits who do not understand their true purpose would seek to interfere negatively in the life of someone on earth. All cases of spirit possession (known to psychologists as multiple personality problems) and obsession are examples of this type of destructive interference. The cure for mental diseases lies ultimately in the full restoration of mind–body unity centered on God's will and complete resurrection of fallen spirits.

Fallen nature attracts low spirits. Conversely, spiritual maturity attracts high spirits. Low spirits try to dominate people on earth, exacerbating the effects of their fallen nature, whereas high spirits serve those on earth, reinforcing the power for goodness of mature persons. Thus the direction and value of someone's life determines the type of spirits that will associate with him or her.

If a low spirit opposes a good person on earth, that person will experience difficulty in doing God's will. However, through persevering in goodness, he will grow and the spirit itself will be educated. Thus men and women who maintain spiritual maturity and live according to God's principles benefit all those spirits with whom they have relationships: high spirits grow by cooperating with them and low spirits are educated by their principled steadfastness and can grow by applying what they learn.

Conclusion

Restoration, or salvation, is accomplished when men and women take responsibility for their lives and willingly offer themselves to God. Through this offering of self, they are able to make a foundation of faith and a foundation of substance, and, as purified human beings, be prepared to receive true parents. The main goal of restoration history has been the creation of a foundation for true parents. Only once true parents come can Satan's dominion of evil be ended and the world of God's original ideal realized.

When individuals make indemnity conditions for restoration, their fallen spirits are resurrected from the death of separation from God to life in oneness with God. Thus the history of restoration has also been a history of resurrection. The progress humankind makes in this history is determined by the level of human effort. Without people making a total commitment to a life of faith, the restoration/resurrection process cannot advance. To counter the lack of faith in fallen humanity, God has sent many messengers and prophets with the mission to bring enlightenment and to encourage renewed efforts in the preparation for true parents.

The principles of restoration explained in this chapter can best be understood in their historical application. They are not just a set of abstract theories but are rather the very means by which fallen humanity is purified of sin and by which the history of restoration moves forward. The explanation of history that is contained in the following chapters shows how these principles have operated in the lives of providential individuals, families, tribes and nations. As a first step, this account returns to the archetypal family of Adam and Eve, which is discussed in the next chapter.

10 | ADAM'S FAMILY

INTRODUCTION

The principles of restoration operate in all human affairs, affecting every life. Consequently, they have been the inner dynamic of human history, shaping the destiny of individuals, families, tribes and nations. The theory of their operation was explained in the previous chapter. The practice will now be examined.

The fall of Adam and Eve severely damaged their characters and set them on a path of suffering and misery. As their loving parent, God must have anguished over their plight, even though they were responsible for it. No time could be lost, the work of restoring Adam and Eve had to be started at once. Thus Adam's family is where the fall took place but also where the providence of restoration was begun. The operation of the principles of restoration can be seen in the developments that took place in Adam's family after the fall.

Adam Divided: Cain and Abel

After falling, Adam and Eve lost their capacity to respond directly to God because they were torn between the good impulses of their original natures, inclining them to God, and the bad impulses of their fallen natures, inclining them to Satan. Being in this mid-way position, with no one to guide them on the path back to God, they were unable to separate themselves from the domination of Satan to begin the process of restoration.

That is why God began the restoration process in the second generation of Adam and Eve's family. They had three sons: Cain, Abel and Seth, born in that order. The two oldest were chosen to make conditions for restoration. The basis for this choice was as follows. Fallen Adam's nature was divided into two parts: his original nature as Adam the obedient son of God, and his sinful nature (acquired from the servant) as Adam the disobedient servant of God. In effect, the two parts of Adam's divided nature were represented separately by his two oldest sons: Abel represented the original Adam and Cain represented the Servant.

By this externalizing of the divided nature of Adam, God set up the circumstances for Cain and Abel to make conditions to restore the Adam and Servant relationship and through that process to purify themselves. Both sons inherited fallen nature from their parents, but by loving each other as true brothers their original natures would prevail against the inclination of their sinful natures. If, on the other hand, they allowed themselves to be dominated by their fallen natures, Cain, as the Servant, would seek to control a submissive Abel, and the mistakes of the fall would be repeated.

Why was Cain, the first son, put in the position of the Servant and Abel, the second son, put in the position of Adam? Cain, as the first-born, represented the fruit of the first love relationship of Eve, with the Servant, while Abel represented her second love relationship, with Adam. From God's point of view, her second relationship was relatively better than her first because in the first Eve submitted to the Servant's domination and, through subsequent relations with Adam, transmitted that submission to Adam and her children. In the second relationship, her motivation included the desire to return to God through union with Adam, who was to be her husband. It was an immature relationship rather than a fundamentally unprincipled one.

Furthermore, the eldest son was originally the natural heir to inherit God's true life, love and lineage from his parents. Because of the fall and Satan's usurpation of God's position, however, Cain became the child who naturally inherited the satanic life, love and lineage of his parents. Because Adam and Eve submitted to the Servant, Satan could make a claim on Cain as the first fruit of Adam and Eve's fallen union. This meant Satan's influence was more powerful over Cain than over Abel, making it difficult for Cain to respond to God and easier for God to work with Abel. Thus, because Cain was the oldest son and represented the more unprincipled of Eve's fallen relationships, he was born as the representative of the Servant. Abel, as the second son, was born as the representative of Adam.

The Foundation of Faith

The responsibility of Cain and Abel was to make indemnity conditions to restore the mistakes of their parents as a foundation for true parents to come. The first step in making this foundation for true parents was to establish faith, to lay a foundation of faith. Cain and Abel were called upon by God to offer as sacrifices their best produce and livestock, respectively. Cain's sacrifice was rejected by God, whereas Abel's was accepted. God's acceptance of Abel's sacrifice signaled Abel's success in laying a foundation of faith (i.e. he had responded faithfully) and confirmed him as the representative of unfallen Adam in the second generation of the first family.

The Foundation of Substance

When Cain's sacrifice was rejected he felt intense jealousy towards his successful brother. Cain resented the fact that Abel, the younger brother, had been favored by God. Cain's position was similar to that of the Servant who was created before Adam and Eve and had witnessed God's growing love for them as they grew in maturity. Cain's desire to be the channel for God's love and to dominate Abel was similar to the Servant's desire when he sought to dominate Adam and Eve.

Like the Servant, Cain could not contain his unprincipled jealousy which boiled over into a fit of rage against his brother, whom he attacked and killed. In murdering Abel, Cain repeated the sin of the Servant, who spiritually murdered Adam and Eve. Cain succumbed to the influence of his sinful nature instead of gaining dominion over it, and thus repeated the fall instead of reversing it. Cain should have acceded to the divine decision and accepted the choice of Abel as God's representative. If Cain had humbled himself to Abel, he would have received God's love and blessings through Abel.

Thus although Abel was successful in laying a foundation of faith, the possibility of establishing a foundation of substance through cooperation between Cain and Abel was lost when Cain killed Abel. The reversal of the fall and purification of the fallen nature could have been accomplished only if Cain, in the position of the Servant, had been willing to submit to Abel, in the position of Adam. The murder of Abel meant that the opportunity to lay a foundation for true parents in Adam's family was lost once and for all.

Cain's action represented Satan's will but Satan cannot pervert or destroy God's creation beyond a certain limit because God is the sole creator of all beings and He has the ultimate dominion over creation. By the principles of creation God will not let Satan claim more than any one creation can take from another. Therefore, Satan can never destroy the God-given original nature of another being and cannot ultimately succeed in his efforts to destroy God's original plan for an ideal world.

Nevertheless, because Cain had submitted to Satan and Abel had been killed, God had to choose an alternative to Cain and Abel to begin restoration. Seth, the third son of Adam and Eve, was chosen by God as the man to keep alive the promise of restoration. He became the ancestor of the lineage out of which God selected a family to replace Adam's in the dispensation of restoration.

Lessons from Adam's Family

When Cain killed Abel, the fall of Adam's family was irrevocably sealed, plunging the first human ancestors deep into the realm of Satan. Out of Adam's lineage came all the adulterers, murderers and criminals who have turned God's world into Hell. The problems of Adam's family are the core problems of the world today and have been the fundamental reason for human misery throughout history. Thus the process of the fall in Adam's family, including the transmission of fallen nature from parents to children, contains many lessons of providential importance.

First, one can see how deep-seated the fallen nature was in Adam and Eve. Their fall from knowing God was so total that they created a family environment completely devoid of true love. This became all too clear when Cain killed Abel. It is only in the most depraved families that a son could kill his brother.

Second, one can see in Adam's family how fallen nature is passed from one generation to the next. Even though Adam and Eve, Cain, Abel and Seth were all endowed with original nature, when Adam and Eve disobeyed God and established a relationship of false, ungodly love, this unprincipled behavior was inevitably inherited by their children. The Satan-centered, selfish love of Adam and Eve became the norm for their whole family and its lineage. Once the Servant had abandoned his position as teacher of truth to Adam's family, and their parents had submitted to Satan rather than God, there was no one to educate the children about God and how they could fulfill their responsibilities to Him. They only had the fallen model of their parents as a standard for their own lives. This problem became the problem of all humankind. Generation after generation has grown up without knowing God's will and God's ideal for life.

Third, men and women should be brothers and sisters to each other before they are blessed in marriage. If Adam and Eve had maintained a brother–sister relationship, the damage caused by the Servant's invasion could have been limited and Eve restored. After reaching full maturity as brother and sister, they would have qualified to receive the marriage blessing and would have entered into a relationship of conjugal love with the full participation of God in the creation of their family.

Fourth, since God's will for humanity is absolute, there is always an alternative way forward when a particular individual or group fails its restoration mission. Thus when Cain killed Abel, God chose the third son, Seth, to carry on His providence of restoration. God must prevail in the end.

Fifth, when providential figures are unable to fulfill the missions given them, a prolongation of the providence of restoration always results. If Cain and Abel had succeeded in laying a foundation for true parents, the providence for restoration would have immediately progressed to the next stage and the third generation of Adam's family could have seen the appearance of true parents. They would have set up a sinless lineage and ended the world of evil and suffering before it had a chance to develop. As it was, because Satan claimed Adam's family, the providence was prolonged for many centuries before God could raise up another family in its place. All the suffering and all the sins committed during those centuries had to be restored. With every passing moment the restoration providence becomes more complicated and difficult.

Sixth, both Cain and Abel have a responsibility to fulfill in restoring the relationship between Adam and the Servant to the original order. Cain has to make an effort to unite with Abel, and Abel has to show true love to Cain so that he can willingly surrender to God's representative. Only when both Cain and Abel make a sincere effort towards true reconciliation can purification of fallen nature take place in both of them.

Seventh, resolution of the Cain-Abel relationship, and then the Adam–Eve relationship, is the key to world peace. Conflicts between individuals, families, tribes, nations and blocs of nations are all manifestations of the conflicts within Adam's family. The path of restoration for all conflicts begins with the reconciliation of Cain and Abel, centered on God's will. Thus the process of establishing a foundation of substance, in which Cain willingly surrenders to the love of Abel, is the model course for peace-making between all enemies. Once a foundation of substance is completed, a foundation for true parents exists and the Adam–Eve relationship can be restored. Once true man-woman love is established, a new lineage is created and individuals, families, tribes, nations and the world can be restored, creating a world free of Cain–Abel conflicts altogether. In this way a world of true peace will be realized.

Eighth, the path for Cain to return to God is through Abel. The only way the servant can win the heart of his master is by helping the master fulfill his dreams, namely raising up a worthy heir. The secret of the servant's glory is in serving the son. Cain represents the Servant, Lucifer, Abel the son, Adam. Abel qualifies for the son's position by being obedient to God and by being willing to sacrifice himself for others. Fallen men and women need to find Abel figures to serve and thereby attract to themselves the love and gratitude of God. The ultimate Abel in the fallen world is restored Adam, the true father who, with true mother, establishes a true family. Thus fallen people can only complete their return to God through sinless true parents.

Ninth, God gives His blessing to Cain through Abel because in restoration He does not have relations with the representative of Satan directly, only with the relatively purer side. After the Servant lost his position as teacher of Adam and Eve, he no longer had the right to approach God directly. He had no qualification to do so. Because Cain represents the fruit of Adam and Eve's disobedient behavior, if God were to bless Cain directly, it would be as if he blessed the fall, giving fallen relations eternal value. God blesses Abel as a representative of good, and, when Cain unites with Abel, blesses Cain through Abel.

Tenth, since Adam's family is the archetypal fallen family, wherever there is evil in the world it reflects an aspect of the fallen natures of Adam's family. Therefore, one can see in all human temptations a resemblance to the temptations experienced by Adam, Eve and the Servant. And all the struggles people face in pursuing a good life are struggles to remove the fallen tendencies inherited from the first ancestors. By knowing what happened in Adam's family, repetition of the mistakes that led it into Hell can be avoided. Every fallen man is tempted, as the Servant and Adam were, to leave his position in order to engage in illicit love; and every fallen woman is tempted, as Eve was, to leave her position in order to engage in illicit love. To understand the origin of temptation and sin is to gain the weapon with which one can overcome temptation.

Eleventh, Satan's greatest strength lies in his invisibility. It is hard for sensible, earth-bound men and women to believe that Satan is real. No doubt Cain was such a sensible person, and didn't recognize Satan in his own anger against Abel. Fallen human nature makes a base for invisible Satan to work, inciting resentment and hatred, lust, anger and violence. Satan has a hold on fallen humanity through the fallen lineage of Adam's family.

Only by understanding the presence of this base inside themselves can fallen individuals act to counter the influence of Satan in their lives.

Conclusion

The more people understand the mistakes made in Adam's family the more they can recognize the root causes of evil in the world. The sins of the first human ancestors are repeated again and again in the fallen world, with individuals, families, communities and nations acting out the unprincipled patterns of behavior they have inherited from the first family. Only by knowing the root cause of evil can people work effectively to eliminate it from their lives.

The pattern of inheriting fallen nature was established in Adam's family when Cain and Abel were born with the behavioral characteristics of their parents and repeated their parents' mistakes. Purification of Adam and Eve's lineage was not achieved by their children, but their descendants paid indemnity so that God could choose a new family to represent Him on earth. That family was Noah's. It came from the lineage of Seth and it had to restore the failures of two generations of Adam's family. The providential story of Noah's family is the subject of the next chapter.

11 | NOAH'S FAMILY

INTRODUCTION

The fall of Adam's family set humanity on a long, dark course of indemnity before God was able to choose a family out of the lineage of Seth to restore Adam's. That family was Noah's. Its mission was to indemnify the mistakes made in Adam's family and lay a foundation for true parents, who would begin a new lineage of sinless men and women. According to scriptures, the time period between the two families was 1600 years (4 x 400) spanning the course of ten providential generations. Ten is the number that represents return of humanity from its fallen state to full unity with God, after passing through nine stages of growth.

The Foundation of Faith

God worked through these generations to create a man of good character and humility. Noah was called by God to make an offering as a condition to establish once again a foundation of faith. He was instructed to build an Ark, a large, three-decked boat, and to load it with representatives of the creation in preparation for a massive flood. The Ark represented the whole cosmos, with Noah's family in the position of humankind. By separating Noah's family and the Ark from Satan's world, God could begin the restoration providence again, with a pure family and a representation of nature: all the elements needed for fulfillment of the three blessings.

Noah had great faith in the word of God and invested himself completely in building the Ark, even though the people of his time, including his own family, found it ludicrous to build a huge boat on a mountain when there was no evidence of a flood to come. It took Noah a very long time to complete the project, but in persevering he succeeded in making a foundation of faith.

Because of Noah's great faith God chose his family to prepare for true parents and the creation of a new, sinless lineage. God inundated the land with a 40-day flood, allowing only Noah's family and the animals he brought on board the Ark to be saved from destruction. The flood physically separated Noah's family from the fallen world, giving Noah a chance to set up the conditions for true parents to come to a purified world.

The number 40 represented the four position foundation being restored through ten generations, so the flood indemnified the 1600 years and ten generations from Adam to Noah. The 40-day flood set a pattern of indemnification through 40-based time periods. Consequently, these time periods appear frequently in religious history.

The Foundation of Substance

Noah's family had eight core members, after the pattern of Adam's. Noah had three sons, Shem, Ham and Japheth, representing Cain, Abel and Seth respectively; Noah's wife represented Eve and his three sons' wives represented the wives of Adam's three sons. The first generation of Noah's family had to restore the first generation of Adam's, and the second generation of Noah's family the second generation of Adam's. Therefore Noah was chosen by God to lay a foundation of faith to restore Adam's lost faith and renew the faith of Abel, but his two sons had to make a foundation of substance to restore the failure of Cain and Abel. By Shem and Ham restoring the relationship between Cain and Abel they would make a condition to restore the relationship between the Servant and Adam.

Ham as the second son was naturally in the Abel position because, as in Adam's family, Satan had a stronger claim on the first son. Nevertheless, Ham had to make a condition to inherit the foundation of faith from his father so that he could be confirmed in the Abel position. Unless he was united in heart with his father's realm of faith, indemnifying the passing of fallen nature from parents to children, Ham could not qualify as Abel.

However, when his faith in Noah's devotion to God was tested by an apparent moral lapse on the part of his father, Ham proved wanting. He was embarrassed by the sight of his father lying unclothed in his tent. Ham got his brothers to cover their father. On waking from his sleep, Noah was angry with Ham. Noah knew that by covering him Ham was being critical and that this criticism came from a lack of faith in him, even though he had demonstrated incredible faith in building the Ark at a time when everyone was ridiculing him. At root, Ham's shame at the sight of his father's naked body showed that he was still under the influence of the fall. Shame in the naked human body was introduced by Adam and Eve when they covered their sexual parts after misusing them in the fall. Ham showed that he was not free of that fallen influence and therefore was not qualified to inherit the foundation of faith from his father. Furthermore, even though Noah's faithfulness had saved Ham's life, Ham was not persuaded of his father's godliness. Instead, in a shameful display of arrogant self-righteousness, he urged his brothers to condemn the very person whose faith had saved them.

Because Ham failed to inherit Noah's foundation of faith, he could not take the Abel position in relation to his elder brother, Shem. This meant they could not even begin to create a foundation of substance. Thus Noah's family was invaded by Satan and was unable to restore Adam's family. This meant the providence of restoration had to be prolonged so that indemnity could be paid for the failure of Noah's family as well as the mistakes of Adam's family.

According to the pattern of Adam's family, Satan wanted to claim dominion over Noah's sons through Shem, the first born. However, when Ham acted against the will of God and his father he took Satan's side, allowing Satan to invade Noah's family through Ham. According to the principles of creation and restoration, Satan cannot claim everything from God's side. Therefore he could not dominate both Shem and Ham. Once Ham had been taken by Satan, God claimed Shem, the firstborn. Because of Ham's failure, Shem was never put in the Cain position. Out of the lineage of Shem God chose a new family to lay a foundation to restore Adam's family. That was the family of Abraham.

Lessons from Noah's Family

Noah's family contains several important lessons for people, especially in the consequences of Ham's loss of faith in his father. Although his father had conditionally restored Adam's faith by building the Ark, Ham had no foundation of faith himself because he had not supported his father in the construction of the Ark. It was natural of Ham's fallen nature to suspect the faith of Noah, but if Ham had looked at his father from a God-centered perspective he would have recognized him as a great man of faith. Sometimes Cain cannot understand the words or actions of Abel because Abel's perspective is more vertical, or God-oriented, than Cain's. This means that Cain has to learn to trust that God is working through Abel, even though he may not understand how.

The key lessons to be learned from Noah's family follow. First, God's restoration providence is often difficult to understand and therefore Abel figures should be supported in the providence because they are chosen to represent God's point of view. God's providence of restoration is always centered on Abel. If Abel is successful, the providence can succeed through harmonious cooperation between Cain and Abel. If Abel is unsuccessful, there is no way for Cain to succeed. Ham should have supported Noah as the Abel figure of his family until Ham himself was qualified to inherit the foundation of faith from his father and establish a foundation of substance with Shem. By disuniting with Noah, Ham destroyed the providence for his family.

Second, because of his position the Abel figure is often endowed with insights into God's providence which are important for the success of the mission. Abel is the person God is most likely to communicate with to get a message to fallen humans. Thus Noah received instructions from God (to build the Ark) that others in his society, including his own family, considered patently foolish. They should have trusted that Noah's closeness to God made it possible for him to have a particularly profound understanding of God's will. Thus Abel's potential for greater insight has to be trusted by Cain.

Third, since every fallen man and woman has a Cain-like nature inherited from the fall, everyone must find an Abel figure to guide him or her to God's providence and a virtuous life. No person can restore his or her own fallen nature without the help of Abel. Because fallen nature entered human beings through unprincipled relationships between irresponsible individuals, the only way to remove it is through principled relationships between responsible people. Abel represents the position of Adam before the fall, that is principled and responsible Adam. This is true even though within the fallen world Abel, as a fallen person, is merely the one who is relatively closer to God than Cain. Ultimately, though, sinless true parents are the perfect guides for fallen people to return to God because they have an absolutely true, godlike perspective. They must be followed humbly by those who seek to leave behind the world of Satan's dominion.

Fourth, following an Abel figure is training to follow the absolute Abel, true parents. Their explanation of God and standard of life is bound to be much higher than normal levels and therefore incomprehensible to many. Only by following them in the faith and knowledge that they are indeed the true representatives of a responsible and principled life, in the position of Adam and Eve before the fall, can one inherit their understanding and their restored standard of love, life and lineage.

Many of the lessons of Adam's family are also repeated in Noah's. For example, one can see again that if a person chosen for a certain mission is unable to fulfill that mission, another will take his or her place. Ham was chosen to represent Abel, but instead Shem, who was originally to have restored Cain, became the Abel of his generation and the ancestor of God's chosen people. It is also abundantly clear in Noah's family that the failure to establish a foundation for true parents resulted in a significant prolongation of the restoration providence with a further multiplication of sin and suffering.

Conclusion

The dominion of Satan over humankind established in Adam's family resulted in centuries of human suffering before conditions were set for Noah to be chosen to restore Adam. However, despite Noah's great faith in building the Ark, Satan was able to invade his family through the faithlessness of Ham. Thus Noah's family lost its chance to be the starting point of a new, restored history.

Ham's mistake resulted in a 400-year prolongation of the providence of restoration, after which God chose Abraham to restore the families of Adam and Noah. The four providential generations of Abraham's family are the subject of the next chapter.

12 ABRAHAM'S FAMILY

INTRODUCTION

Four hundred years and ten generations passed after Noah before sufficient conditions had been laid for God to choose a family to restore the mistakes made in the families of Adam and Noah. The central person God chose was Abraham, and Abraham's family was given the task of laying foundations of faith and substance. Four generations of Abraham's family contributed to making successful foundations for true parents and launching a new dispensation of restoration which eventually grew from the individual to the global level.

Because of this success, Abraham was a prophet of special importance. His family became the starting point of the lineage chosen to receive true parents. He and his descendants received revelations from God which gave birth to the three great monotheistic religions: Judaism, Christianity and Islam.

However, even though Abraham was such a great providential figure, not all went well in his family. Because it is human nature to err in the fallen world, several mistakes were made which caused delays and complications in the dispensation of restoration. Some of the problems sowed seeds of discord that multiplied into tribal, global and national rivalries and conflicts, seriously damaging God's providence. This chapter will explain the successes and failures of Abraham's family and how these affected the providence.

Preparation for Abraham's Mission

Abraham's most important qualification to become a prophet and to lay a foundation for true parents was his lineage. He was chosen out of the descendants of Shem, a lineage which had been blessed by God after Satan had claimed Ham. Much indemnity was paid in Shem's lineage, making a foundation for Abraham. Without special preparation and help of this nature, it would be impossible for a providential figure of Abraham's stature to fulfill his God-given mission.

In the history of restoration, anyone chosen to be a central figure in the providence of God must first qualify for the mission by separating from the fallen world. This purification process confirms the central figure in his mission and readies him to participate in God's work. Only after a central figure makes conditions to purify himself and devote his life to God will God use him in the providence.

Although Abraham came from a blessed lineage, his own father worshiped idols and created a home environment dominated by Satan. Abraham had to separate himself from this fallen environment before he could begin his mission for God. In Noah's providential course, the chosen family was separated from the sinful world by the flood; in Abraham's case he was called by God to leave his home and travel to a land that would be shown to him as the place where he should settle and lay the foundations for a sinless family.

Abraham obeyed God. He rejected the idolatry of his father and left his homeland in Chaldea with his wife Sarah and nephew Lot. Sarah, who represented Eve, had not yet given birth, so Lot stood in the position of their child at that time. With the help of God, Abraham's family travelled safely to its destination in Canaan, overcoming all obstacles along the way. In a final attack from Satan, Egypt's pharaoh tried to seduce Sarah in a repetition of the Servant's seduction of Eve, but he was warned of the consequences and, out of fear, allowed Abraham's family to leave in safety. Having successfully separated his family from the internal fallen world of his home and the external fallen world of Egypt, Abraham was ready to make conditions to establish a foundation of faith.

The Foundation of Faith

God called on Abraham to make a sacrifice. Making this offering woul lay a foundation of faith. Abraham was to take a heifer, ram, she goat, pigeon and turtle dove, cut them in half and offer them to God. Abraham cut the animals in half, but not the birds. This minor error provided an opportunity for Satan, represented by the birds of prey, to invade the offering, with two consequences. First, Abraham was called upon to make a condition of greater indemnity by offering his son in place of animals and birds, and, second, he was told his descendants would have to undergo a 400-year period of slavery to indemnify the error.

By not cutting the birds in half, Abraham failed to make the necessary condition of purifying the sacrifice before it was offered to God. Before being cut, the whole sacrifice was under the dominion of Satan, much as Adam after the fall. And in the same way that Adam had to be divided into Cain and Abel, the sacrifice had to be divided, conditionally separating Cain from Abel in the offering, draining out the fallen blood and separating the fallen elements from the good.

The birds, male and female, represented man and woman in the formation stage of restoration; the ram and she goat represented man and woman in the growth stage and the heifer represented the unified being of man and woman in the completion stage. In making the offering, Abraham was setting up a condition for the restoration of humankind through the three stages. When the birds were not cut, Satan was able to invade the foundational formation stage of the sacrifice, thus claiming the whole offering.

Abraham was determined to restore this mistake, and, despite the incredible difficulty, he prepared to sacrifice his son, as God had asked him. Before doing so, he once more had to pass through a process of separation from Satan, who had invaded his family through the failed sacrifice. His family was again subjected to a trial similar to what it had experienced in Egypt, but this time it was King Abimalech who tried to seduce Sarah. As with the pharaoh, the king was warned by God that he would be punished if he kept her and in fear he returned Sarah to Abraham who then left Abimalech's kingdom safely. Abraham's family had once more separated itself from Satan and was prepared to lay a foundation of faith.

Abraham Offers His Son

God instructed Abraham to sacrifice his son. (According to the Bible he prepared to sacrifice his second son, Isaac, who was the only child of Sarah. The Koran does not specify which son it was but Islamic tradition generally holds that it was his first son, Ishmael, born of his servant Hagar. According to the pattern of restoration demonstrated by the Principle, it is always the second son who, as Abel, has to offer himself to restore Adam's faith.) Father and son traveled for three days to reach the mountaintop location appointed for the sacrifice. Abraham prepared an altar of firewood on which to offer his son. He was just about to pierce the body of the boy when an angel intervened to stop him, telling him that his faith was sufficient.

Abraham's great faith in being willing to offer his own child as a sacrifice to God restored his family as the central family for God's providence. Most important, his son accepted what his father was doing, believing that it was the will of God. It is hard to imagine how the youth could be so obedient as to cooperate with his father in his own death. By showing this incredible faith, a condition was made to restore Ham's loss of faith in his father Noah and to establish a foundation of faith in Abraham's family.

On the strength of this victory, Isaac, as the second son in Abel's position, was fully united with his father's heart of faith and was able to take the place of his father in fulfilling the foundation of faith. He assisted in offering a sheep as a sacrifice. Thus, on the strength of two successful foundations of faith, made by Abel and Noah, and the great faith of Abraham in offering his son, Isaac inherited his father's position as the central figure to restore Adam's faith. This made him, like Noah and Abraham before him, a father of faith.

The Foundation of Substance

According to the principles of creation, human beings are the central figures of creation and all other beings are created to be objects to them. Therefore, the Servant, although created before

Adam, was to be obedient to Adam and receive God's blessings through Adam. In the fall, the Servant took unrighteous dominion over Adam through Eve. Because of this reversal of positions in the creation, God would not give His blessings to Adam or the Servant. To bless them when they were violating the principles of creation would have been to accept an unprincipled relationship as principled, giving it eternal value.

According to the principles of restoration, the relationship between Adam and the Servant has to be restored to the proper order by a representative of the Servant willingly submitting to a representative of Adam. After the pattern of restoration established in Adam's family, the older son is chosen to represent the Servant and the second son to represent Adam. Once the relationship between Adam and the Servant is righted by Cain submitting to the love of Abel, a foundation of substance is achieved and both Cain and Abel can receive the blessings of God.

If Abraham had completed the foundation of faith himself, then his two sons, Ishmael and Isaac, would have been responsible to restore the Cain-Abel relationship and lay a foundation of substance. If successful, both sons would have received the blessings of God. But because of the mistake in Abraham's first offering, Isaac inherited the position of father of faith from Abraham, and his two sons, Esau and Jacob, inherited the positions of Ishmael and Isaac (Cain and Abel).

Ishmael and Isaac

As the older son and child of a servant, Ishmael was to have restored the Cain position and received God's blessings through unity with Isaac. But after Abraham's position had been passed to Isaac, Ishmael was not able to participate with his brother in laying a foundation of substance and could not receive the blessings that God had promised to give the sons of Abraham. As both the Bible and Koran confirm, the history of restoration from Abraham's family initially developed in the lineage of Isaac. His son Jacob became the father of faith to 12 sons who became the 12 tribes of God's chosen people, the Children of Israel. Only many centuries later, with the advent of the prophet Mohammed, did the lineage of Ishmael come to play a central role in the providence of restoration.

Therefore, due to no fault of his own, Ishmael was excluded from participating in the immediate providence of Abraham's family. The blessing promised to Ishmael and his descendants was inevitably linked to the providence of Isaac, since God viewed Abraham's family as one lineage. Ishmael's difficult position was conducive to his feeling resentful for having to wait to receive God's blessing. The tendency to feel resentful towards Isaac and his lineage was passed from Ishmael to his descendants and has been one of the providential problems needing restoration. Ishmael had twelve sons whose offspring became twelve tribes of the Arab people. It was to fulfill His promise to Ishmael and to end the historic resentment between the families of Isaac and Ishmael that God eventually sent Mohammed to the Arabs some 2500 years after Abraham's family had passed into the spirit world. (See Chapter 19.)

Resentment destroys human relationships because it is predicated on the desire to take what others have for oneself rather than to give of oneself to others. It is destructive both for its target as well as for the person who harbors it. Resentment was a major motive behind the Servant's rebellion against God and invasion of Adam and Eve's love relationship. It can only be overcome by the power of love, which confirms the original value of its object and liberates fallen humanity from resentments, enabling people to fulfill their potential. Thus the descendants of Isaac and Ishmael were to love each other in order to resolve the resentment planted in Ishmael's heart and heal the divisions that grew out of the inability of Isaac and Ishmael to unite in the providence of Abraham's family.

Jacob and Esau

Like their father Isaac and uncle Ishmael, Jacob and Esau were especially important figures in the history of restoration. For this reason, considerable space is devoted to them here.

Esau and Jacob were twins, with Esau the first-born. Jacob, in

Abel's position, had to win Esau's willing surrender, even though Esau, representing Cain, enjoyed the privileged position of first son. As a fallen man, Esau's natural inclination was to dominate Jacob against the will of God, but in the end Jacob was able to persuade his twin brother to accept him as God's representative and together they succeeded in laying a foundation of substance.

There were several steps in achieving this victory. Jacob first won the birthright from Esau by offering a meal in exchange for it at a moment when Esau was hungry and valued food above his position in the family. Esau's attitude was like that of fallen Adam, who set personal gratification above the purpose of establishing a good lineage, whereas Jacob understood the superior value of lineage.

Forty years later, when Isaac was old and blind and on the verge of death, Jacob succeeded in winning his father's blessing in place of Esau. Rebecca, Isaac's wife, assisted him in this, thereby restoring Eve's deception of God and Eve's failure to secure God's blessings for her children.

Esau was furious when he discovered that Jacob had received the blessing that was to have been his as the oldest son. His jealousy and anger towards Jacob were similar to the feelings of the Servant towards Adam and Eve when he felt he was losing the love of God. They were also similar to the jealous feelings of Cain which prompted him to murder Abel. Jacob did not want to give his elder brother an oppportunity to murder him, so, again with the help of his mother, he fled to the home of his uncle Laban, in Haran.

Laban was a Servant-type figure whom Jacob had to win over with service and love. Jacob served Laban for seven years to win the hand of his daughter Rachel. But Jacob was cheated by Laban who substituted Leah for her sister Rachel on the wedding night. He worked a second seven years to win Rachel, whom he then married as well.

When Jacob wanted to return home, Laban would not let him take any material goods with him, even though Jacob had served Laban faithfully for fourteen years and made him rich. So Jacob worked a third seven years to win material wealth. By persevering in loving and serving Laban until he gained a victory, Jacob conditionally restored Adam's subject position over the Servant. On the foundation of this success he also won dominion over the material world, thus completing conditions to fulfill the three blessings: restoring himself, his spouse and possessions.

On the strength of this victory, Jacob returned to his homeland in Canaan. On the way back, at a ford crossing the river Jabbok, he encountered an angel, who wrestled with him. Even though the angel dislocated Jacob's thigh, Jacob persevered and eventually prevailed against the angel. Once again, Jacob had restored the proper relationship between the Servant (the angel) and Adam (himself). By not giving in to the angel, Jacob made a condition to reverse the fall. Having won the contest, he demanded the blessing of the angel, which he received, together with the new name Israel, which means 'he who strives with God'. From this point on, Jacob was known as Israel and his descendants as the Children of Israel.

After his victories over Laban and the angel, Jacob continued towards Canaan and prepared to meet his brother Esau, who, still angry over having lost the birthright and blessing, was preparing to attack him. Jacob understood the anger and resentment in Esau's heart and wisely offered Esau his wealth and all that was precious to him before they met. Esau, who had expected to face his brother returning as a conqueror, was surprised and moved by this generosity and love. When Jacob himself appeared, Esau forgot all his anger and the two brothers embraced in tears. Jacob had completely won the heart of his brother Esau.

The loving reunion of Jacob and Esau restored the Cain-Abel relationship and, for the first time in the dispensation of restoration, a foundation of substance was successfully completed by a providential family.

The Foundation for True Parents

Abraham's was the first family chosen by God to restore Adam's family in which both a foundation of faith (by Isaac, inherited by Jacob) and a foundation of substance (by Jacob and Esau) were laid successfully. The moment when Esau and Jacob embraced in love was the most hopeful and joyful moment for God after the fall of Adam and Eve. With that great providential success, a foundation for true parents had finally been achieved and God could begin to build the providence of restoration on a substantial level, expanding His foundation among the fallen people of the world.

However, true parents themselves could not appear at that time because Abraham's error in the sacrifice of the animals and birds had first to be restored through Jacob's family and descendants. The indemnity period for this restoration was the 400 years of Israelite captivity in Egypt. Furthermore, by Abraham's time Satan had dominion over whole nations whereas God had only one family on His side. How could one family succeed against nations?

Perez and Zerah

The reconciliation between Jacob and Esau was a major victory for God. Nevertheless, it was not complete indemnification of the fall since it represented only a symbolic purification of blood lineage. the substantial purification of lineage had to be accomplished in the womb, which is where fallen nature entered into humanity.

This is what lies behind the paradoxical story of Tamar. By understanding that Tamar like Isaac's wife Rebecca, was in the position to restore fallen Eve, one can know why Jesus was born of her lineage, out of the tribe of Judah. She risked her life when she obeyed God's instructions and bore twins by her father-in-law Judah who was one of Jacob's sons.

At the time of birth, the position of the twins was reversed in the womb, such that the younger son, Perez, representing Abel, was born before his brother, Zerah. The reversed order of birth was known because Zerah's hand had emerged before Perez was born, and a red thread had been tied to it before it was retracted into Tamar's womb.

The purification of Tamar's womb was the foundation for Jesus to be born sinless, which is the primary qualification for the messiah. As messiah, Jesus was to become a true parent and establish a purified lineage, free from Satan's dominion to God's dominion by grafting into the lineage of true parents.

Jacob's Lineage is Chosen

When Jacob and Esau restored the relationship between Cain and Abel, they completed the first foundation for true parents in history. Therefore God chose the descendants of Jacob, who became the twelve tribes of Israel, as the people to establish a nation to receive the messiah. When Tamar restored the purity of Eve's womb, God chose the lineage of Judah to give birth to the messiah. Thus Abraham's family, and in particular Jacob's lineage, became the beginning point for the expansion of the restoration providence from the individual to the family, tribe and eventually, national foundations to receive true parents. And the Children of Israel became the chosen people.

Jacob's Family Foundation

Jacob's family became the center of God's providence. Jacob had 12 sons, the first ten by three women: Leah, the servant of Leah and the servant of Rachel. The two youngest, Benjamin and Joseph, were by Rachel. These 12 sons created families that became the 12 tribes of Israel, the people chosen by God to be the nation to receive the true parents.

The internal, Abel-like attitude of Jacob was inherited in particular by his second-to-last son, Joseph. The brothers of Joseph were envious of his position as a favored son of Jacob and they sold him into slavery in Egypt. There Joseph prospered and became prime minister under the pharaoh. By overcoming temptations of the fallen world of Egypt, especially the seduction of women, Joseph was confirmed as the Abel figure in the second generation of Jacob's family.

When famine struck Canaan, his homeland, his brothers came to Egypt to purchase grain. He recognized them and, despite their terrible mistreatment of him previously, he received them with love, giving them grain and returning the money they had used to purchase it. They could not understand this generosity, but when they went on a second grain-buying mission to Egypt Joseph revealed his identity to them. The brothers wept with joy to be reunited.

Joseph used much the same wisdom in winning over his brothers as his father had employed in gaining the love of Esau. By giving his brothers gifts, he showed that he loved them even though they had done him wrong in the past. For their part, they were willing to repent and ask forgiveness for what they had done to him. By this restoration of the Cain-Abel relationship in Jacob's family, the individual foundation for true parents established by Jacob was expanded to the family level by his sons.

Lessons from Abraham's Family

First it is important to pay attention to detail, in addition to having a willing heart, in the completion of indemnity conditions. Fallen people are not able to fulfill the original responsibilities of sinless Adam and Eve completely because their sinful nature is incapable of responding fully to God. To accommodate this limitation, God made it possible for fallen individuals to fulfill their responsibilities conditionally by making offerings of nature and themselves. Thus making an offering to God is a conditional fulfillment of human responsibility, a step towards the substantial fulfillment of responsibility by restored men and women. The need to make offerings came about because Adam and Eve did not complete their responsibilities as God's son and daughter: they failed to take God's warning seriously and, consequently, failed to carry out God's instructions diligently. Therefore, an offering only has meaning if it is completed with the right heart of responsibility and the diligent implementation of instructions.

Abraham was serious about fulfilling his responsibility to God in undertaking the offering of animals and birds, but after finishing the major portion of his offering by cutting the animals in two, he somehow overlooked the much smaller task of cutting the birds. From this small mistake, Satan was able to invade the whole sacrifice.

The gravity of the situation created by Abraham's omission mirrored the fundamental reality of the fall. On the face of it, one could say that the mistakes of Adam and Eve in the fall were minor when judged against the evils of the fallen world. And yet those seemingly minor mistakes were the cause of all human suffering and misery. A small mistake can have major consequences if the person making the mistake is a central figure on whom many depend. Adam and Eve were the first human ancestors and all humanity was affected by what they did. Abraham had the mission to establish a foundation for the restoration of all humankind. His error affected everyone in his lineage and all those touched by it in the providence of restoration, which, ultimately, was the whole world. In both cases, because of the great providential importance of these central figures, the failure to complete God-given responsibilities was the cause of great difficulties for the whole of humanity. If God asks for something specific, people should assume that it is important, even if they cannot understand how or why from their limited perspective.

Second, an attitude of total humility and obedience to God is the most powerful weapon against Satan. Complete humility was demonstrated by Abraham's son in accepting his father's decision to obey God by sacrificing him. His unconditional willingness to offer his life for the will of God completely defeated Satan's plan to destroy Abraham's family. There was no room for Satan in the relationship between Abraham and his son because both were committed to obey God at the cost of their lives. It would have been easier for Abraham to offer his own life than to kill his beloved child. Their powerful demonstration of faith made it possible for Abraham's family to retain the central providential position that had been put in jeopardy by the mistake made in the earlier offering.

Their faith represents the ultimate standard of faith, a level of commitment that restores Adam's lost faith. In the fall, Adam was killed spiritually when he ignored God's warning about the consequence of eating the fruit. He sought to gratify his own desire at the cost of his life. He could not see the absolute importance in something that seemed inconsequential from his narrow point of view. Restoration of Adam's wrong attitude is accomplished when someone in Adam's position sacrifices his own desires for the will of God, even at the cost of his life. It is this willingness to obey God completely, at any cost, that facilitates God's ability to give all, including life, to the one with such faith. Therefore, because Abraham's son was willing to die for God he did not have to die.

Another lesson of great importance is the need for Abel to win the heart of Cain through service and love. Jacob was the first Abel figure in the history of restoration to succeed in laying a foundation of substance because he made a great effort to melt the resentment and anger of Esau by giving love to him even in the most difficult circumstances. The mission of Abel is to win the willing surrender of Cain. Only love can achieve this and service is the practice of love. Jacob's son Joseph learned well from his father and won his brothers' hearts by serving them with love even though they had acted in an evil way towards him. Both Jacob and Joseph were able to win the willing cooperation of Cain (Esau and the eleven brothers, respectively) to establish foundations of substance, moving the providence of restoration forward significantly.

Conclusion

Abraham's family was the beginning point of the expansion of God's providence of restoration. Abraham and the three generations of his family that came after him all played important parts in creating the conditions to make this possible. Out of Abraham's family came the peoples who were chosen by God to bear the major responsibility for the restoration providence: Jews, Christians and Muslims.

With the second generation of Jacob's family having made the family foundation for true parents, the providence focused on expanding this foundation to a national level. By the end of the four centuries of slavery suffered by the Children of Israel, Moses was sent to Egypt to liberate them and to set up a national foundation for true parents. The life of Moses and his role in God's providence are the subject matter of the next chapter.

13 | Moses and Judaism

INTRODUCTION

When the family of Jacob first left Canaan to join Joseph in Egypt it numbered 70. After 400 years it had grown to number some 600,000 males, over one million people in all. Although enslaved by the Egyptians, God intended to use them for the building of a nation to receive true parents. That nation would be God's settlement on earth, the place where His dominion would prevail and from where the ideal would be expanded to the rest of the world.

To accomplish this nation-building mission the Israelites had to leave captivity and return to the land of their forefathers, Canaan. According to the principles of restoration, a national foundation has to be built on foundations laid for individual, family and tribal restoration. Thus the Children of Israel needed a leader who could liberate them from captivity in Egypt and set up a family and tribal foundation for the creation of a nation under God.

Moses was the man chosen by God for this mission. He was to lead the Israelite slaves out of Egypt and into the promised land of Canaan, where they were to establish a theocratic state. Accomplishing this mission proved extremely difficult because the Israelites had grown accustomed to life in Egypt and were reluctant to sacrifice what they had for the uncertain promise of their own nation, even though their lot as slaves was miserable. Because of the faithlessness of the Israelites, Moses had to go through the work of establishing a national foundation three times. Each time Moses had to lay a foundation of faith to qualify as the Abel figure for the whole nation of Israel and then win the trust of the

Israelites, who collectively stood in the position of Cain to him, to lay a foundation of substance. Each of these efforts represented a providential course of restoration, a series of events through which God worked to establish a true nation.

The First National Course

Moses was the son of an Israelite family but he was adopted by the daughter of the pharaoh and was raised as a prince in the pharaoh's palace. He was educated in the Israelite tradition by his real mother, who stayed in the palace as his wet nurse. Thus although Moses grew up in the heart of the satanic world, he was secretly educated about God and told of the instructions and promises God had given Moses' ancestors. At that time, there was no written record of revealed truth to be transmitted from generation to generation, only the oral record of God's dealings with the families of Adam, Noah and Abraham as well as some lesser figures in the providence. Part of this oral tradition included God's all-important promise to Abraham, namely that He would multiply and bless the great patriarch's descendants. The Israelites clung to the hope that God would eventually bless them as the children of Abraham.

One day, when Moses was 40, an argument between an Egyptian overseer and an Israelite slave broke out, putting Moses in a position to demonstrate his true loyalties. He killed the Egyptian, showing that despite his royal position he identified with the Hebrew slaves. This was a sign for the Israelites to recognize Moses as the liberator they awaited. But they failed to see their savior in Moses, prince of the palace. Moses soon fell under suspicion in the palace for having favored a slave over an Egyptian, and when his true identity was discovered he was forced to leave Egypt for exile in Midian.

Through maintaining his faith in the one true God of Abraham during his 40 years in the palace of the idolatrous pharaoh, Moses succeeded in laying a foundation of faith on the national level. However, the foundation of substance was not established because the Israelites did not recognize and accept him as their Abel figure.

The Second National Course

Moses spent 40 years in Midian, all the time keeping his faith in God. He worked for the Arab Jethro, and married one of his daughters, Zipporah. At the end of the 40 years, God called him to return to Egypt to liberate the Israelite slaves. After some hesitation, Moses took up the mission for the second time.

Moses went to the pharaoh's palace to demand the release of his people. The pharaoh was unwilling to let them go, so God gave Moses three signs with which to convince him. These miraculous signs also served to show his people that he was the leader they had been waiting for. When the demonstrations of God's power, failed to move the pharaoh, Egypt was afflicted with ten calamities that brought great suffering to the Egyptians and eventually persuaded pharaoh to allow the Israelites to leave.

The Egyptians depended on the services provided by the Israelite slaves and the Israelites themselves were accustomed to life in Egypt, despite its discomforts and difficulties. Because of this it took many dramatic displays of God's power to bring about a clear separation between Egypt and the Children of Israel. From a providential point of view, the Israelites needed to realize that they had to completely separate from their old life in Egypt in preparation for creating a God-centered nation in Canaan. So long as they had longings for their past life under Satan's dominion, they could not respond fully to God's will for the future.

When the pharaoh finally permitted them to leave, they crossed into Sinai. Moses had the tremendously difficult mission of leading over a million people through the desert to Canaan, the land promised to them by God. They had no written laws to govern the affairs of the 12 tribes, let alone those of a nation, and they had no experience of self-government as an independent people. They needed a minimum set of laws and a basic structure for their society while they were in transition from a state of slavery under a pagan regime to theocratic statehood.

To meet this need, God led them to Mount Sinai, where He called on Moses to lay a foundation to receive His instructions. Moses fasted for 40 days on Mount Sinai to establish a foundation of faith, and afterwards received ten commandments on two tablets. But when he returned to the people he found they had lost faith and reverted to the worship of Egyptian gods, preventing the formation of a foundation of substance to receive the word of God.

Because the Israelites failed to make a foundation to receive God's word, Moses smashed the two tablets in anger, destroyed the idols and instructed the Israelites to repent and return to God. He then climbed Mount Sinai again and once more made a 40-day fast. Again he received ten commandments on two tablets, but he had to hew them from the rock himself this time. When he once more returned to his people, he found that they had remained faithful to God, thus completing a foundation of substance. The foundations of faith and substance laid at Sinai by Moses and the Israelites together made a foundation for true parents. Because there was no national foundation established as yet, true parents came in the symbolic form of the word of God, written on two tablets.

Ultimately, God wants to send true parents in the flesh, as the word incarnate, because only a sinless man and woman can finally defeat Satan and liberate fallen humans from sin. However, at the time of Sinai the foundation for true parents was not sufficient for them to come in more than a symbolic, representative manner. One must remember that before Jacob successfully laid a foundation of substance with Esau, there was no foundation at all for true parents; and that once the foundation had been established in Jacob's family the condition of 400 years' slavery, indemnifying Abraham's error, had to be completed before God would send true parents in any form. To facilitate preparation of a nation, God gave Moses the Ten Commandments on two tablets, representing the messiah and his bride to come.

Moses was also given instructions for construction of a tabernacle, a portable temple for use by the Israelites during the transition from their life in the old, fallen world of Egypt to their new life in Canaan. The Tabernacle was designed with an outer sanctuary, called the Holy Place, and an inner sanctuary, called the Most Holy Place. With its inner and outer parts, the Tabernacle was a symbol of the true man and true woman to come, with inner spirit and outer body. Once the Israelites had settled in Canaan they were to build a temple in place of the Tabernacle, as a more substantial precursor of, and foundation for, true parents.

Moses was instructed to place the two tablets in a special Ark of the Covenant, which, together with the staff of Aaron, would be kept in the Most Holy Place in the Tabernacle. These objects represented the true parents to come. By centering their lives of faith on them, the Israelites would prepare to center their lives on true parents. And by demonstrating their obedience to the Tabernacle and the Ten Commandments they would show their obedience to God. Moses himself set an example for the people by giving utmost respect to the Tabernacle and its holy contents and by obeying the Ten Commandments.

From Mount Sinai the Israelites continued on their way to Canaan, travelling through the inhospitable desert. The difficulties they faced made many of them regret they had ever left the relative security of life in Egypt. Many lost sight of the vision of a promised land and fell to complaining about their situation. Without that vision to inspire them, they lost the power they needed to complete their nation-building mission.

Because of the grumbling, Moses set up a new condition to reestablish the people's faith before attempting to enter Canaan. He selected one person from each tribe to go on a 40-day spying mission in Canaan. When the 12 spies returned, ten of them counseled against proceeding with the plan to invade Canaan, advising instead that they all return to Egypt. But two, Joshua and Caleb, said they believed that with God's help the Israelites would be able to prevail in Canaan, despite the formidable strength of the Canaanites. This agreed with Moses' position. He understood that God wanted the people to enter Canaan by all means. Turning back would negate the value of all the efforts that had brought them that far. However, most of the Israelites united with the ten spies who advised a return to Egypt, thus rejecting the position advocated by Moses.

In effect, this meant that the Israelites had once more disunited with Moses. Consequently the foundation of substance in the second course could not be completed successfully. God told the Israelites that because of their lack of faith they would not be allowed to enter Canaan at all, but would instead have to pass through an indemnity period of 40 years in the desert, after which only the new generation would be allowed to enter Canaan.

The Third National Course

During the Hebrews' 40 years in the desert, Moses, in the Abel position, remained faithful to God, for the third time setting up a successful foundation of faith. But when, towards the end of this period, the people demanded water to drink, Moses lost his temper at their complaining and in anger struck the rock at Horeb two times to produce water for them. By this time, Moses had struggled with the faithlessness of the Israelites for so long he could not contain his anger at them. But this was an error since according to God's instructions only one blow was needed.

The ire of Moses blocked God's providence because God still depended on the Israelites to set up a true nation, and Moses, representing God, had to continue to love them and lead them for God's will to be fulfilled. Moses had shown his anger before, when he smashed the two tablets, but striking the rock in anger was more serious, since the rock symbolized God, whereas the two tablets, taken from rock, symbolized true parents.

Because of this error, Moses was told that he would not be able to enter Canaan himself, but would only be granted a chance to see it. Because of his three great foundations of faith, the Israelites would indeed reach the land promised them by God, where they would set up a nation to receive true parents. Nevertheless, a condition was made for Satan to invade the leadership of the Israelites, resulting in a prolongation of the providence to build a temple and receive the true parents. Instead of this taking place within Moses' course, it was postponed for 400 years to the time of King Solomon. This postponement was similar to the 400-year prolongation of the providence which resulted from Abraham failing to cut the birds of his sacrifice.

Joshua

Before dying, Moses climbed to the top of Mount Nebo and looked out over the lower Jordan valley and the Dead Sea to the promised land of Canaan. Prior to this he selected Joshua to stand in his place as Abel to the people and as the man responsible to complete a foundation of substance in the third course. Joshua was selected because he had been completely faithful to the Tabernacle and the law, and had been united with Moses throughout the Israelites' ordeal in the desert. To restore the lost spying condition, Joshua sent two spies into Jericho, a mission they completed successfully, opening the way for the Israelites to enter into Canaan. Thus Moses' mission to lay a national foundation for true parents was eventually completed by Joshua in the third course.

Joshua's victory opened the way for the 12 tribes of Israel to settle in Canaan and establish a nation there. Their mission was to build a temple to replace the Tabernacle as the central object of their worship and to create a national society governed by the laws of God, given through Moses. To accomplish this, the 12 tribes were to unite with the central figure appointed by God, who was Joshua. He campaigned hard for the realization of a unified Jewish nation in Canaan, both by carrying out military campaigns to subdue the Canaanite kings and by trying to unify the disputatious tribal chiefs of Israel. However, he faced considerable resistance on both fronts and when he died his successors lacked his zeal in the mission. Soon the Israelites lost sight of their central mission and got bogged down in petty inter-tribal issues. Many abandoned their hard-won tradition and adopted the pagan practices of the Canaanites. This resulted in a prolongation of the providence to build a temple and receive true parents.

Judaism

In the course of restoration centered on Moses, for the first time ever fallen humanity was given the word of God in the form of revealed truth. Before receiving this revelation of truth, humankind had lacked an articulation of God's will to guide men and women on the path of restoration. They had wandered aimlessly in the wilderness of their own ignorance for centuries, unable to find the way forward to the fulfillment of their purpose.

Beginning with the Ten Commandments, the Children of Israel were given specific instructions for their lives. Out of these the beliefs and practices of the religion of Judaism were shaped.

Modern Judaism is rooted in Mosaic law but enriched by centuries of revelations, insights and scholarship.

Each religion offers its own special perceptions of God and provides a basis for a life of faith, giving it an eternal value that transcends time and place. Judaism, as the first truly monotheistic faith, is the elder brother of Christianity and Islam and contains the essential truths on which those two global religions are founded. Judaism, like all religions, awaits its completion through the true parents, who together fulfill the mission of the messiah.

Furthermore, the Jewish contribution to human civilization is enormous. Jews have been prominent in literature, art, philosophy, economics and science, in many cases leading in these fields.The quality of Jewish culture has provided the foundation for this tremendous flourishing in many areas of human endeavor.

Lessons from Moses' Course

First there is a need for payment of greater indemnity when a condition is unsuccessful. Because of faithlessness among the Israelites, the second attempt to set up a national foundation for true parents was more difficult than the first, and the third more difficult than the second. Moses' course in the pharaoh's palace was relatively easy, as was the responsibility of the Israelites, who merely had to accept Moses as their leader. In the second course, Moses went through 40 difficult years in Midian to lay a second foundation of faith, and the people had to suffer through many trials and tribulations to be separated from the Egyptians and to reach Canaan. But the third course, in which Moses and the people had to survive in the desert for 40 years, was by far the most difficult.

Second, a providential leader has to take responsibility for the failures of his followers if God's dispensation is to advance in his lifetime. Representing Abel to the people, Moses had to take responsibility for their many mistakes by laying new conditions that enabled God to continue to work with them as His chosen people. For example, when they refused to accept him in Egypt, he had to suffer exile and go through a 40-year period of indemnity to remake a foundation of faith, even though the primary responsibility for the failure for the first exodus providence lay with the Hebrew slaves and not with Moses. And, again, when the people lost faith during his first 40-day fast on Mount Sinai, he prayed for their forgiveness and returned to the mountain for a second 40-day fast, so that he could once more receive the Ten Commandments for the people. His whole life was devoted to saving the Israelites even though their behavior on the surface indicated that they neither wanted to be saved nor appreciated what Moses had done for them. A leader in the providence of restoration must expect to make indemnity conditions for his followers, regardless of their lack of appreciation. It is a willingness to sacrifice for others that qualifies someone as a central figure in the dispensation of restoration.

Third, Moses' life shows that if a central figure maintains his position by fulfilling the conditions called for by the providence, he can continue to be used by God even if those he is responsible for fail their responsibilities. Moses, as Abel, laid foundations of faith only to face faithlessness among the Israelites. Nevertheless, when one course was cut short because the Israelites would not follow him, Moses set about laying a foundation for the next course. His position and mission as Abel was not changed by the failure of Cain. Only when the faithlessness of the people led him to make a mistake did he lose the Abel position, which passed to Joshua.

Fourth, restoration is accomplished in three stages: symbol, image and substance. This follows the pattern of creation in which God made nature first, which embodied His essence symbolically, and then created human beings, in His image. Mature human beings and the rest of creation together comprise the substantial incarnation of God. In Moses' course, true man and woman were restored symbolically as the two tablets of stone inscribed with the word of God, encapsulated in Ten Commandments. The two-part Tabernacle was a symbol, and the temple to replace it was an image of a true person. Substantial restoration was to be accomplished by a man and woman in the flesh.

Fifth, the course of Moses demonstrates the need for law as well as a leader. The law embodies the will of God for fallen people and keeps them on the path of restoration even when there is no leader to do so. Before and after Moses, there were many centuries during which there was no one to guide humanity through the pitfalls of the fallen world. Before Moses, there was no law to fill the leadership gap; after Moses, the laws he brought guided the children of Israel on the right path. Should a leader in the providence make a mistake due to his fallen nature, the law will not be destroyed. Ultimately, the laws of God prepare humankind to receive the perfect embodiment of God and His laws, the true parents.

Sixth, Moses' course shows the importance of setting up a tradition for some future purpose to be fulfilled. The Hebrews were instructed to erect a Tabernacle so that they could be trained in a life of faith centered on one central figure. The tradition of loyalty to the Tabernacle was created to qualify the Israelites to receive true parents who would replace it and the temple as living embodiments of God's law. To be saved, the Israelites would have to devote their lives to God through obedience to true parents.

Seventh, followers need to trust in their Abel's greater understanding of God's invisible providence. Moses showed a faith in God's dispensation that was not shared by most of the other Israelites. He believed that all would work out to their benefit, as promised by God, even though at times their situation was desperate. Regardless of the setbacks and difficulties they faced, Moses persevered in his mission, convinced that the Israelites were participating in God's providence. It is easy for someone in the fallen world to lose faith in God's dispensation for restoration, because fallen humanity is surrounded by more evil than good. This reality has caused great difficulties for the central figures sent by God. Usually they are rejected by the very people they seek to help. Thus Moses was repeatedly rejected by the Israelites even though he demonstrated the power of God working with him; Jesus was also rejected by his own people, even though his life was a model of devotion to God; and Mohammed was rejected by the people of Mecca until his successes in Medina showed that God was working with him. The central figure of any providence is given greater insight into God's plans because God has chosen to work through that person for the benefit of the whole. Followers have to trust their leaders' greater understanding of God's dispensation and demonstrate faith accordingly.

Eighth, providential leaders must develop parental hearts if they are to express God's love to people and avoid making mistakes. A central figure should only express anger at evil itself and not at the people God wants to save from evil. The heart of a true parent may be angry at an evil act of a child but will always maintain love for that child and work for his salvation. The course of Moses reveals that anger was his one real short-coming. His anger at Horeb was directed at the people themselves and not just the specific lack of faith they displayed. This unparental rage had destructive consequences for Moses and the Israelites.

Conclusion

Through making tremendous efforts in three attempts to liberate the Hebrew slaves and establish a God-centered nation, Moses virtually dragged the Children of Israel out of their Satan-dominated environment in Egypt and through the inhospitable desert of Sinai to the promised land of Canaan. At the end of his life, Moses passed the mission of establishing a nation for God to Joshua, who became the first leader of newly-founded Israel.

However, the internal objective of creating a purified and unified nation centered on a temple was not completed by Joshua, and the providence was prolonged for four centuries before Israel was united under a king with the mission of building a temple. Even after the temple was built by Solomon, a series of mistakes by providential leaders and their followers resulted in a further prolongation of the dispensation so that it was a full millennium after Solomon before Jesus came as the promised messiah to fulfill the mission of true parents. The history of Israel from Joshua to the coming of Jesus is the subject of the following chapter.

14 | ISRAEL

INTRODUCTION

Moses led the Israelites out of captivity in Egypt to build a God-centered nation in Canaan, a nation prepared to receive true parents and lead the world back to God. This chosen nation was called Israel. The history of Israel is the history of a struggle to establish a settlement for God's people in the midst of the fallen world. The mission was especially difficult because no pattern existed for a God-centered nation and the institutions necessary for its development. The problems faced in nation-building resulted in several delays in God's providence, delays which occurred when mistakes were committed by central figures and their followers in Israel. Eventually, 16 centuries passed before a foundation was finally set up for true parents and Jesus was sent as the long-awaited savior, or messiah. The reasons for the prolongations in the providence of Israel are explained in this chapter.

400 Years of Slavery

The period of slavery in Egypt, discussed in the previous chapter, was necessitated by incomplete conditions in Abraham's family. The Children of Israel suffered under the secular rule of the pharaohs to pay indemnity for those mistakes and to lay a foundation to receive a central figure who could establish a national foundation for true parents. The awaited liberator and national leader was Moses.

400 Years of Judges

The Israelites were to settle in Canaan and build a temple to replace the Tabernacle. The central figure had the mission to unify the 12 tribes in a theocracy centered on the temple. The first step in this direction was to unify Canaan politically, which the invading Israelites attempted by subduing the Canaanite kings. Joshua was the first central figure of Israel and he is said to have been personally responsible for the death of 31 rulers of various parts of Canaan. In the meantime, the tribes took control of territory on both sides of the Jordan river.

Despite his best efforts, Joshua was unable to unify Israel. Tribes tended to pursue their own interests rather than contribute to building the nation. Furthermore, the Israelites' lack of faith in God and their tendency to mix socially and religiously with the pagan Canaanites, sometimes through marriage, resulted in the Jews losing sight of their real purpose in Canaan. As a people guided by God, theirs was the Abel position in Canaan, but they became confused about their own beliefs. As Abel they were to love the Canaanites, winning them to God's side through service and education in the truth of God. However, without clear spiritual understanding and conviction they could not accomplish this.

Joshua was the first judge over the people of Israel, combining the roles of king, chief priest and prophet. He was followed by eleven other Judges, the last being Samuel. The 400-year period of Judges was marked by ongoing conflicts between the various tribes and with other peoples in the lands they sought to settle. The Israelites increasingly wanted a strong political leader to unite the tribes against common enemies and establish a strong kingdom.

120 Years of the United Kingdom of Israel

The last Judge, Samuel, responded to the peoples' desire and anointed Saul as the first king of Israel. Saul ruled Israel for 40 years, but was not successful in protecting the nation from its enemies. Neither was he able to build a temple to house the Ark of the Covenant, the two tablets and the staff of Aaron.

David succeeded Saul as king of Israel on the strength of his faith in God and courage in battle. He was a prophet as well as a king, and he authored many beautiful songs praising God. But David spent most of his 40-year rule securing Israel against its enemies. Because he had shed so much blood, David was not allowed by God to build a temple.

That mission was passed to David's son, Solomon, who, in the fourth year of his 40-year reign, began building a great temple. Once completed, the Temple of Solomon was a magnificent testimony to the Israelites' devotion to God. As king of Israel, Solomon was to unite the 12 tribes with the Temple and its holy contents.

But Solomon neglected this all-important mission. He married 700 wives and took an additional 300 concubines. He began to worship their gods, in some cases compromising his own faith and the faith of his people by allowing the erection of altars to the idols worshiped by his women. How could the Israelites be expected to unite around the one true God and the Temple if their leader himself was not setting an example of faithfulness? Through his loss of faith, Solomon failed to complete the foundation of faith and qualify as Abel for the nation of Israel.

Externally, Israel itself was well-qualified for the mission of chosen nation at that time, achieving its highest level of development as a leading power in the area. This national-level success was given to Israel by God so that it could accomplish the pivotal task of receiving and protecting true parents and expanding their foundation to the world-wide level. But Solomon's fallen relations with women, through which Satan invaded his foundation of faith and polluted the purity of the Temple, led to the destruction of God's providence centered on the United Kingdom of Israel. Solomon's error compromised Israel so that it had to be purified through division. Consequently, Israel was split into two nations.

400 Years of the Divided Kingdom

When Adam fell, he had to be 'divided' into Cain and Abel for his lineage to be purified. When Solomon failed, his kingdom was divided into the northern kingdom of Israel, with ten tribes under his servant Jeroboam, and the southern kingdom of Judah, with two tribes under his son Rehoboam. The division took place so that the fallen elements within Israel could be separated from original elements and the kingdom purified. The southern kingdom was in the Abel position and the northern kingdom in the Cain position.

Judah's mission was to win Israel back to God's way through love and education. To accomplish this, several prophets were sent to the north to teach God's truth and wean the northerners from their idolatrous practices. But despite the power of God demonstrated by these prophets, the people of Israel did not repent and return to God. Their disobedience made a condition for Satan to invade them, and Israel was attacked and destroyed by the Assyrians, some 240 years after the death of Solomon. The ten tribes were scattered and to this day are called the lost tribes of Israel.

Despite all the efforts of the prophets, Judah itself eventually adopted the evil practices of the north, in particular idolatry. Because of this, the southern nation could not fulfill the foundation of faith as a purified Abel and the two kingdoms could not be united to make a foundation of substance to complete a national foundation for true parents.

210 Years of Babylonian Exile and Return

Because of its defilement, Judah was invaded by King Nebuchadnezzar of Babylon. Jerusalem was sacked, the Temple of Solomon destroyed and the holy objects (the Ark of the Covenant, the two tablets and the staff of Aaron) were lost forever. Thus ended the Kingdom of Israel, founded by Saul, built up by David and divided on the death of Solomon. The evil of idolatry that Satan had used to undermine the faith of Israel was not expunged from the midst of the Israelites in the course of the four centuries of divided kingdoms. Therefore Satan was finally able to claim the whole of what had been Solomon's Israel when the remnants of the tribes of

Judah and Benjamin, who had been the nation of Judah, were taken as slaves to Babylon. They where kept in captivity for 70 years.

The destruction of their kingdom and temple and the harshness of their captivity shocked the Israelites into realizing how far they had strayed from their purpose as builders of God's chosen nation. Nevertheless, despite their mistakes, God still wanted to use them for that purpose, having given them the lineage and the truth needed for restoration. When they repented deeply for their sins and begged God to allow them to return to Jerusalem, God was moved by their purified attitude and forgave them. They were finally liberated when a Zoroastrian king, Cyrus the Great of Persia, conquered Babylon, freed them from captivity and allowed them to return to Jerusalem. The return to Israel took place in three stages over the course of more than a century.

In Jerusalem, the reconstruction of the Temple was accomplished and the Hebrews recommitted themselves to the founding principles of Israel: the laws revealed to Moses. Israel was re-established as a theocratic state, having been purified of idolatry through its indemnity course in exile. The whole period of Babylonian exile, return to Israel, reconstruction of Jerusalem and the Temple and restoration of the theocratic state took 210 years.

400 Years of Preparation for True Parents

Israel then embarked on a final 400-year period of preparation for the true parents. During this era the chosen people paid tremendous indemnity to qualify for the blessing of being the first nation restored. Israel was conquered by the Persians, Greeks, Egyptians, Syrians and Romans, the last in 63 BC. Only during a single century of Maccabee rule did Israel enjoy any real independence from foreign control. The national tribulations of Israel heightened the longing of the Jewish people for a savior, the messiah. The prophets had told of his coming, but it was four centuries after the last great messianic prophecy, that of Malachi, before Jesus was sent to fulfill the mission of the promised messiah, the mission of true parents.

Conclusion

The first 1600 years of the history of Israel as a nation, from its founding by Joshua to the coming of Jesus, is a record of struggles to achieve national unity and purity in the face of internal dissension and external attacks. Israel, as the nation chosen to receive true parents, had to prepare for its mission by becoming a principled state, governed by God's laws. Frequently during those centuries the Children of Israel lost sight of their purpose as they sank into pettiness and squabbling. To rectify this and keep the providence moving towards its goal, God sent many prophets and other Abel-type leaders to put the people back on the right track. Eventually, sufficient conditions were laid for God to send Jesus as the messiah with the mission to establish the Kingdom of Heaven on earth, beginning with the people of Israel. (His mission and life are discussed in Chapter 17.)

During the final period leading up to the coming of Jesus, Israel was not alone in preparing for true parents. The rest of the world was experiencing an unprecedented era of enlightenment, with developments in all areas of human endeavor. Since the mission of true parents is to save all of humankind, every culture contains internal elements that provide a foundation for receiving them. The next chapter outlines the global preparations for the realization of God's ideal on earth, centered on Jesus.

15 GLOBAL PREPARATION FOR TRUE PARENTS

INTRODUCTION

After the Israelites rebuilt the Temple in Jerusalem and recommitted themselves to obey the word of God, there was a final 400-year period of preparation for the coming of true parents. This four-century period was to restore the 400 years of Judges and the 400 years of divided kingdoms. Both of the earlier periods had been invaded by Satan, preventing the creation of a purified nation qualified to receive and follow true parents.

Since the mission of God's chosen family is to free all humankind from Satan's dominion, the providence preparing for its coming, although centered in the lineage of Jacob, ultimately embraced all peoples. In the time period before Jesus came, God worked through prepared individuals and groups in several parts of the world to raise the consciousness of people everywhere to accept the messiah and his bride. This work of global preparation began when the Israelites in Babylon truly repented for their sins and determined to return to the true faith of Moses. Their repentance made a condition for God to initiate worldwide spiritual renewal and to connect all humankind to the central providence of Israel.

In East Asia God raised up the philosophers Lao Tzu (604–531BC) and later Confucius (552–479BC) to provide a principled social order through which people could prepare for the heavenly social order centered on true parents. Confucius understood the providence of God as the Mandate of Heaven and, living like a prophet, he urged leaders of his time to conform to ethical laws.

In the Indian subcontinent God sent Buddha (563–483BC) to add important principles to the foundation of Hinduism and to provide understanding of the path of growth to perfection and purity which must be trod by those who wish to fulfill their true purpose. Buddha rejected the Hindu worship of idols and by denying the material world made himself a true object of God, so that he could be enlightened by God's love and truth.

Zoroastrianism flourished in Persia and introduced important concepts about God to the people living in the geographic area between the monotheistic Semites and the adherents of Eastern spiritual paths. Zoroastrianism influenced the providence of Israel when Cyrus, a devotee, conquered Babylon and freed the Hebrew slaves.

Even when explained in outline, each of the world religions that developed during this period can be seen to contain important insights about God and the creation. Even though the expression of these truths often differed from monotheistic teachings, the new religions served to complement the revelations given to Jesus later on.

The development of religions during this period was complemented by a number of significant developments in other areas, such as science and technology, politics and economics. This chapter will look at some of these non-religious preparations for the advent of true parents, and the following chapter will look at the global religious preparations.

Greece

In Greece, God nurtured a civilization which developed many important concepts and principles for organizing society, nations and the world. Led by the great philosophers Socrates (470–399BC), Plato (427–347BC) and Aristotle (384–322BC), the ancient Greeks contributed theories of science, society, politics, education, medicine and law that have had a lasting impact on the world. Religion addresses the realm of spirit, but people also need to understand their bodies and the physical world, the province of science. The ideal world will be one of harmony between spirit and body, religion and science.

The Greeks played a critical role in the development of science, establishing it as a major force in human development and founding many of the branches of knowledge that have become essential parts of the scientific corpus. They explored the mathematical and philosophical principles that underpin art and science, developing the basis for the scientific method itself, which derives from Socrates' method of proceeding to knowledge through hypothesis and deduction. Aristotle added induction, based on experimentation.

The Greek approach to knowledge was not divorced from religious belief but it relied more on observation and speculation than on faith. It focused on the tangible person and the visible world known to humankind, rather than the invisible world of spirit. To the extent that religious beliefs influenced Greek theories of humanity and the universe, they were based on a polytheistic faith that assigned particular powers and functions to gods in the Greek pantheon. In Judaism, these powers would be considered diverse attributes of the one God.

The Greeks made many remarkable discoveries which have held their value to this day. Behind this outpouring of knowledge God was working to prepare the world externally for the fulfillment of the three blessings, through which human beings will gain full dominion over themselves and nature in accordance with the will of God. Without understanding themselves and their environment human beings are incapable of achieving a world of true love.

Merely listing some of the notable figures who contributed to various fields of knowledge (and in some cases founded sciences) gives an indication of the extent to which Greek civilization played a providential role in developing human understanding (all dates are BC):

Philosophy: Thales (640–546), Anaximander, Anaximenes and Heraclitus (6th–5th Centuries), Leucippus (480–410), Socrates (470–399), Democritus (460–370), Protagoras (480–410), Georgias (485–380), Prodicus of Ceos and Hipplias of Elis (5th Century), Antisthenes (444–370), Plato (427–347), Diogenes (412–323), Aristotle (384–322), Theophrastus (372–287), Autolycus (360–300), Epicurus (342–270), Zeno (335–263), Cleanthes (331–232), Chrysippus (280–207), Posidonius (135–51), Zeno of Sidon (150–78);

Mathematics: Pythagoras (582–500), Hippocrates of Chios (5th Century), Aristotle (384–322), Theaetetus and Eudoxus (4th Century), Euclid (2nd–3rd Centuries);

Science/Technology: Pappus (4th Century), Archimedes (287–212), Aristarchus (3rd Century), Hipparchus (2nd Century);

Medicine: Hippocrates (460–377);

Astronomy: Claudius Ptolemy (2nd Century), Aristarchus (3rd Century);

Navigation/Geography: Pytheas (4th Century), Eratosthenes (3rd Century);

Drama: Aeschylus (525–456), Sophocles (496–406), Euripides (484–406), Cratinus (484–420), Eupolis (455–410), Aristophanes (448–380), Philemon (361–263), Menander (342–290);

Literature: Homer (8th Century), Sappho, Alcaeus and Tytaeus (7th Century), Aesop (6th Century), Lysias (456–380), Isocrates (436–338), Aratus (315–245), Theocritus (310–250);

History: Hellanicus (490–405), Thucydides (471–400), Herodotus (484–424), Xenophon (434–354), Polybius (200–120);

Music: Pythagoras (582–500), Simonides (556–468), Pindar (518–438), Bacchylides (516–480);

Sculpture: Polykleitos, Phidias and Myron (5th Century);

Painting: Euphronius and Douris (5th Century);

Architecture: Callicrates, Mnesicles, Ictinus and Polykleitos (5th Century), Dinocrates (4th Century), Pythius (353–334);

Politics (Innovative Rulers): Solon (638–558), Periander (625–585), Pisistratus (554–527), Polycrates (536–522), Aristides (530–468), Pericles (495–429).

Science and Technology

The Greeks not only developed scientific theories, they also studied how to apply those theories in the development of technologies to improve the quality of life. Among these were wood-turning lathes, the lever, wedge, screw, pulley, winch, inclined plane and a gearing system. Cartography, town planning and permanent urban water supplies were also developed.

Greece, and later Rome (which inherited and supplemented much of Greek civilization), also devised various new weapons, such as the torsion engine, the ballista (a siege engine) and the pillum (a balanced throwing spear). They developed cavalry, fast naval vessels (like the Greek bireme and the Roman galley) and armor for soldiers and horses. Iron and steel were used widely in tools as well as weapons, advancing agriculture (the sickle, scythe and the olive oil press, for example) and construction. Greece introduced iron and steel to the West, through Rome. The Romans developed an excellent network of land and sea routes enabling them to communicate throughout their vast empire. In northwest Europe, the iron plough and steerable wagon wheels were developed.

In East Asia, the Chinese made many discoveries during this period as well: piston-billows, canals and dikes, silk scrolls and pointed brushes for writing, draw-looms for weaving, reeling machines for silk working, cable suspension bridges, mat-and-batten sails, rotary winnowing machines and seed-drill ploughs. Alchemy flourished in both Greece and China, and the Greeks produced much of the basic equipment used in science laboratories to this day: stills, furnaces, flasks and beakers. The Chinese produced works on botany and the natural sciences.

Thus the centuries leading up to the birth of Jesus witnessed an unprecedented development in elemental science and basic technologies that transformed the way people worked and communicated. By the end of this preparation period there was a significant unity of civilization in the Mediterranean basin, providing an environment for the introduction of the new culture of true parents, to be established in Israel. The Roman Empire, built on the foundations of Greek philosophy and science, provided the physical foun-

dation that awaited the spirit of an ideal world to be ushered in by
Jesus.

Conclusion

The global flowering of civilization during the period of final
preparation for true parents was driven by religious awakening
and the dramatic development of science and technology. There
was no part of the known world that was not touched, directly or
indirectly, by these developments. The internal dynamic of this
explosive human advance was triggered by the repentance of the
Israelites in Babylon, which enabled God to work more actively
than ever before in the enlightenment of fallen humanity.

However, when Jesus of Nazareth was sent to Israel as the savior
of the world for whom all these preparations had been undertak-
en, he was not accepted by the Jews as the messiah they awaited
and was executed by the occupying Roman army. The reasons for
this tragic turn of events, and the consequences for the providence
of restoration, are explained in Chapter 17.

16 | THE RISE OF ASIAN RELIGIONS

INTRODUCTION

While the Israelites were passing through a period of intense indemnity and spiritual preparation for the coming of true parents, there were parallel religious developments afoot in other parts of the world. These were mentioned briefly in the previous chapter, but need elaboration since the civilizations of Asia shaped by these faiths now embrace almost half the world's population. It is vitally important to know the relationship between these religions and the central providence if one wishes to get a global picture of God's dispensation for the the restoration of all humankind. This chapter examines, in outline form, the histories and beliefs of the major religions outside the fold of Abrahamic faiths, and how they relate to the central dispensation discussed in this text.

All of humanity is nothing other than the single family of God. All people are descendants of the original parents Adam and Eve, who themselves were created by God. Religion became necessary for members of this family only because its founders, the original ancestors, left God and fell into the hands of Satan. Religious history and all history moves toward the moment in which victorious true parents reverse the actions of Adam and Eve, dissolve fallen reality, and establish an eternal lineage connected to God's original creation. It is inevitable that every human being will eventually participate in this final restoration. The immeasurable benefits of restored lineage are not meant for people of only one religion. All true religion must, by definition, have the same goal and purpose, which is to release its members from vulnerability to evil and establish them in an eternal, unbreakable relationship with God. Religions carry out this mission by preparing their followers to engraft on to the family of the perfected original ancestors and become embraced eternally by God. The unique aspect about the Judeo-Christian religious line is that it was used by God to established a purified lineage. By no means can it be reasonably concluded that the blessings resulting therefrom are meant solely for members of that group.

Clan and tribal migrations over time scattered the descendants of Adam and Eve over all available land. The eventual proliferation of population centers and attendant cultural diversity made preparation for a unified Adamic culture more difficult. Nevertheless, in anticipation of the birth and eventual expansion of Adamic culture introduced by Jesus, God and the spiritual world invested in a world-wide program of spiritual instruction and revelation. This spiritual outpouring corresponds to the 400 year preparation period for the messiah. In Judaism that era was given birth by the profound repentance of the Jewish people when they were taken into captivity in Babylon, c.600BC. Repentance led to religious renewal, guided by Ezra, Malachi and other prophetic figures, as well as reconstruction of the Temple and Jerusalem, under the leadership of Nehemiah and other wise governors. Because the messianic providence preparing for Jesus was of global significance, Israel's turning point in Babylon triggered a world-wide movement of religious inspiration and renewal. All regions and cultures were prepared for the advent of true parents by revelations and the leadership of saints who gave birth to the major religious traditions that still exist today.

The reason no new religion, except Islam, has arisen since what is known as the Axial period, is because the pinnacle of spiritual knowledge necessary for human beings to engraft on to the true parents family was already fully given at that time, anticipating the introduction of Jesus' family and culture which would spread through the victorious fulfillment of his mission. When the faithlessness of those prepared to attend Jesus led to his murder, these spheres of near perfect spiritual preparation found in the remaining world's religions, were left unfulfilled. Through them people were elevated to a fully prepared state, ready to make the final step in which they would be permanently released from Satan and united forever with God. The mechanism for taking that final step, however, was thwarted with the abrupt and tragic abortion of Jesus' mission. Over time, when no higher end made itself evident, when the constant spiritual struggle in the world's religions was not relieved by the establishment of Jesus' heavenly kingdom, it came to pass that these religions began to think of their revelations and saints as ends in themselves. When the murder of Jesus ensured continued activity for Satan, God allowed these religions to strengthen themselves and become the purpose of life for the followers in the different cultural regions. In this way God could provide at least some protection for people. In the long run, however, the strengthening of the independence rather than interdependence of religions increased the difficulty of achieving the eventual goal of uniting all people within a single heavenly culture of true parents.

This phenomenal period of preparation for the messiah occurred throughout the civilized world with remarkable coincidence. No adequate explanation has ever been offered for this global phenomenon. In the context of the Principle, however, this period of religious awakening is clearly explained. It is simply God preparing the world for the birth of true parents and the subsequent expansion of the original ideal. God provided visions of truth and love to Zarathustra, sages in the Vedic tradition, Maha Vira, Lord Buddha, Confucius, Lao Tzu and others.

Zoroastrianism

Zoroastrianism, traced to what is now Iran, at one time occupied territories which included Afghanistan, Pakistan, Iraq and, at times, Palestine and Turkey. Zoroastrian Iran was finally defeated by the expansion of Islam, but for over 1000 years Zoroastrianism was the official religion of three major world empires, making it perhaps the most powerful faith of the time. Its later settlement in India is not relevant to our present discussion.

The dates for the Iranian prophet Zarathustra, or Zoroaster, as his name comes to us through ancient Greek writers, are debated.

Those around which greatest consensus occur place him in the 6th
or 7th century BC, around 600BC, within a century of the establishment of the Achaemenid dynasty. The Persian King Cyrus, who
released the Israelites from captivity, was Zoroastrian.

The important thing to note about the founding of this religion
is the radical transformation of the religious environment into
which Zarathustra came. The Indo-Aryan ancestors of the
Zoroastrians likely worshiped a pantheon of nature deities and
featured sacrificial cults attended by a priestly class.

Scholars also debate the vocation of Zarathustra. He is
described by some as a prophet of righteousness, a teacher who in
the name of ethical idealism opposed the degraded popular faith of
Persia. Others see him as a theological innovator, a spokesman for
one God, or, to cite an opposite opinion, a champion of religious
dualism. (This errant latter view will be discussed momentarily.)
Whatever vocation best describes him, records assure us that
Zarathustra was gifted with mystic visions. If he was a moralist, a
social reformer, a theological innovator, he was first and foremost
a prophet and a seer. At the age of 30 he had his first vision of
Ahura Mazda, the supreme God of the Parsi faith, which was followed by six other visions in which six archangels successively
manifest themselves.

Because Zarathustra spoke of an evil "twin spirit" of the one
true God of goodness, the first crude efforts at comparative religion among Western scholars produced the notion of "Persian
dualism." This has since been established as misinterpretation. In
the Pahlavi book, the *Bundahisn*, God enjoys a certain advantage
over His foe from the beginning so that the ultimate victory of
good is insured. Zoroastrianism, despite its dualistic emphasis is
(like Judaism, Christianity and Islam) a monotheistic religion.

It is taught that as we live our lives set in the cosmic encounter
between the almighty Ahura Mazda, creator of all that is good and
who alone is worthy of worship, and Angra Mainyu, the malign
source of violence, evil, and death, we have freedom to choose
between these two powers. The righteous will oppose evil, spread
the good religion of Ahura Mazda, care for the good creation
(plants, animals and fellow human beings) and worship Mazda in
purity. The eternal destiny of human beings is decided by the use

they make of their free will, both at the individual judgement after death and at the universal judgement after the resurrection. The righteous go to heaven and the wicked to hell. With these elements, the powerful record of Zarathustra's own spiritual and practical achievements and the conversion of the Iranian King Vishtaspa, the mighty kingdoms surrounding the small nation of Israel turned from the violent and amoral devas to the exercise of personal responsibility in the effort to worship Mazda.

Hinduism

Hinduism, the religion of the Vedic Aryans, underwent a transformation remarkably similar to the Iranians (Aryans) at virtually the same time. Both Aryan settlements derived from the same period of migration, and both had developed similar religious and cultural aspects in their community by the time of this age of preparation.

Pre-Upanishadic Hinduism was rooted in the polytheism and ritualism of the Vedas (the most sacred Hindu scriptures). Vedic religion was primarily a household religion revolving around Agni, the god of fire. Agni was experienced both in the hearthfire of each home — the fire that cooked their food and warmed their homes, and the mighty Sun (Savitar), the fire that dispelled the darkness of night. Agni was worshiped as a source of fertility in human beings, animals and land.

The other god to whom a large number of hymns of the Rig Veda are addressed is Indra, the great warrior god who led the Aryans to victory and settlement in northern India. Besides Agni and Indra, the Vedic Aryans honored and worshiped a number of other major gods and many minor ones. These gods could make human beings happy if they themselves were made happy. The primary way to achieve this was through the performance of ritual. Two less well known Vedas, the Sama Veda and the Yajur Veda, in many ways served as handbooks for those priests responsible for directing ritual. In the late Vedic period, the time of the Atharva Veda transformed itself to include charms against disease and danger, magical formulas for cursing personal enemies, and then in the later Brahmanas (comment on the Vedas) there appeared verses for bringing about the death of a personal enemy. Thus the use of magic, so sharply rejected in the early books of the Rig Veda, came to be sanctioned.

Even as these significant changes occurred in Vedic religion another development took place. Again these begin to emerge just at the period upon which this chapter focuses. From c.700BC philosophical speculation began to be collected and preserved, some in the form of dialogues between famous sages of the time and their questioners. These collections were called the Upanishads. There was one question above all with which the early Upanishads were preoccupied: Is there one single eternal reality that is the source and essence of the multiform variety of the experienced world? And if there is such an ultimate reality, what is it and how might it be known?

These metaphysical explorations led the sages to identify the ancient idea of the all-pervasive, holy power Brahman as the answer. Brahman was thought to exist independently of the universe, as its source and essence. Of course the strong element of immanence derived from the linked concept of Atman (individual soul) established an enduring interface with a monist cosmology. Nevertheless it is startling to find in this period of global revelation that the great Vedic sages Yajnavalka and Uddalaka Aruni for the first time in ages of Vedic history established a foundation of either monotheism or some related modification of "one ultimate reality that was the source existence and value of the whole world."

In addition to this epoch-making rise of orientation to one ultimate reality, it is also this very time in which the important doctrine of Karma is developed. Again the acquisition of this spiritual principle is attributed to Uddalaka Aruni. It is argued that Aruni received this doctrine from the king of a neighboring territory to the east. Essentially the doctrine of Karma teaches that suffering and happiness are determined directly by one's own actions, in short the necessary foundation and metaphysical moorings of personal responsibility. It must be acknowledged that these doctrines, such as Karma, did not appear in popular Hinduism until later in the Laws of Manu, but the changes were already taking place earlier in the Upanishads.

Equally as important as the infusion of monotheism and the

foundations for absolute personal responsibility, is the end of Indo-Aryan isolation in the region. The Vedic age came to an end with the intensive encounter with the cultures that lay to the east and south of Vedic territory. This advent of theological and cultural exchange can be traced very precisely to 500BC. This significant degree of contact between Dravidian people and the Aryans, who had hitherto kept to themselves, further indicates a synchronicity with global preparations for the birth of Jesus. The first ever period of cultural exchange meant that religious reform and development occurring outside Indo-Aryan territory could spread throughout all ethnic areas. This condition for emerging unification in the region is a necessary element for receiving the Adamic culture without added obstacles of isolation and religious exclusivism.

Jainism

One such development outside Vedic territory was the reformation of Jainism. For eight centuries Jains lived next door to Vedic Aryans. The two communities had virtually opposing religious views, and for all intents and purposes no substantial contact. In the 6th century BC Maha Vira (The Great Hero), the 24th Tirthankara (completely enlightened man) influenced the extant Jain tradition. It was from within this tradition that a rigorous doctrine of Karma developed which empowered the religious call for personal self-discipline and control of physical and fleshly impulses.

The second important contribution of Maha Vira was his strong teaching against the caste system. Here again, the inner impulse which generated this position (apart from the abuses of the Brahmin) was a concern and advocacy for personal responsibility. Maha Vira recognized a Brahmin not by birth but by how he acted. People may be born in a higher or lower caste, but by a life of purity and love a slave girl could be as saintly as a priest.

There is a fundamental transformation of the status of Jainism from the time of Maha Vira. Although 23 Tirthankaras preceded him (the 23rd having been taught c.900–800BC) the record of their appearance, according to Jain teachings, occurred over the course of hundreds of thousands of years. Thus from the perspective of religious history, little of Jainism can be known or considered prior to the 23rd Tirthankara. Today's Jains are entirely oriented to the life and teachings of Maha Vira.

With his life came a dialogue with Indo-Aryan religious thought producing a balance between the transcendent ultimate of the Upanishads and the human response in a state of humility, and personal striving and responsibility.

Buddhism

A contemporary of Maha Vira, although a younger man, was Siddhartha Gautama, called "the Buddha", "the Enlightened One." The rise of Buddhism during the 6th century BC in India parallels the writings of the Upanishads. The life and teachings of the Buddha are far better known than those of the sages of the Upanishads, or of Jaina Maha Vira. The Buddha's biography is an exciting one which results in a simple but challenging doctrine embedded in the Four Noble Truths and the Eight-Fold Path. As with Jainism one finds here a powerful orientation toward human responsibility. (In fact the non-theistic foundations of Buddhism may distinguish it as the most radical of all world religions in the matter of human responsibility.)

The Four Noble Truths define the world view which one must have as a foundation for personal liberation. The Eight Fold Path consists of a tightly conceived system of ethics requiring believers to bear right views, right aspiration, right speech, right action, right livelihood, right effort, right mindfulness and right concentration. This simple program for liberation provides the radical emphasis on human responsibility. Together with the Buddha's (like Maha Vira's) thoroughgoing rejection of the caste system, this creates of Buddhism a powerful force for religious reform.

Buddha denied the efficacy of external rites and ritual sacrifices. Neither bathing in the Ganges nor inflicting self-immolation would serve to purify the believer, according to the Buddha. Buddhism denounced the magic, ritualism and increasing abuses among the Brahmin caste. Together with the fact that it arose simultaneously with the first era of inter-mixing among Aryans and Dravidians makes Buddhism clearly part of global preparations to receive true parents.

One can see through the unprecedented religious ferment on the sub-continent that in each of the great communities the people of the region are elevated to radical new spiritual planes. Throughout the region religious life is time and again turned away from polytheism, ritualism, magic and, at times, even dark and destructive spiritual practices. Through the influences of Zoroaster in the Middle East, the sages of the Upanishads in north-central India and Maha Vira and Lord Buddha to the east and south, these areas are under intense spiritual influences in preparation for the advent of the messiah and the easterly expansion of the true parents' culture of the original ideal.

Taoism

There is great debate about the origins of Taoism, even about the historical existence of its founder, Lao Tzu. From among many hypotheses about him and the seminal text of Taoism, the *Tao Te Ching* (translated either as *The Way and its Power*, or *The Way and its Virtue*), one simply argues that Lao Tzu was a historical figure (604–531BC) and that he wrote the main body of the *Tao Te Ching*.

Taoism, according to scholars, is the religion of "human at-homeness in the universe." Its metaphysics acknowledge the oneness of the ultimate principle which is limitless and beyond rational analysis. Tao is "the Mystery of Mysteries."

The ideal human response to this ultimate is expressed in the elusive concept of "Wu Wei." Successfully applying Wu Wei allows one's inner radiance to shine forth. It is "doing without doing, acting without acting." When one is still, quiet, passive and receptive the Tao itself will act through that person. Wu Wei:

> Can make the small great and the few many
> Requites injuries with good deeds
> Deals with the hard while it is still easy
> With the great while it is still small

Therefore the Sage knows too
How to make the easy difficult, and by doing so
Avoid all difficulties
(Stanza 63, the *Tao Te Ching*)

Here is a religion of humility, self-surrender for the human being and harmony with the natural world. This world-view, grounded in the mysterious oneness of the absolute principle, calling for humility and surrender from its practitioners, has at least one additional element that is readily identifiable as preparation for true parents. This is the strong influence of Yang Yin, the ancient Chinese philosophical principle at the base of all Chinese religion. Yang and Yin describe complementary polarities characteristic not only of male and female interaction but also the harmonization of heaven and earth.

In East Asia, this message combined with the powerful transformation evoked by Confucius, contributed to reform the tragic state of affairs of the Chou dynasty. This age will be examined after a look at the other major contemporary force for reform, Confucianism.

Confucianism

King Fu Tzu (Confucius, the Great Master King) was born 553BC (d.479BC) in Shantung Province, China. Legend describes a meeting between Confucius and Lao Tzu, creating an interesting parallel between the Buddha/Maha Vira encounter. The scope of this chapter does not permit a deep study of these pairings of enlightened teachers at the same moment in history, but the parallels between sub-continental and East Asian religious transformation are remarkable.

Although nine books constitute the primary corpus of Confucianism, it is commonly acknowledged that the *Analects* is a faithful rendering of what Confucius said to his disciples, and basic to understanding his life and thought.

The starting point of Confucius' thought revolves around Hsiao, or filial piety, obedience to elders. This core principle underlies the entire development of a system with values that Confucius rightly believed would result in a good society, a good government and a good life for families and individuals. Grounded in Hsiao, each person, family or leader of large political units should seek to embody five special characteristics, first, Chung Tzu, the qualities of a superior individual, one who is "broad-minded, not small-minded, conciliatory but not flattering, dignified but not arrogant... has a kind expression, respectful manner, and is sincere in what one says." Second, Jen, true virtue, benevolence, good will, "human-heartedness." Third, Li, good manners, propriety and respect at all times (one should approach all things in life with the same reverence, awe and humility with which one performs ritual and offering). Fourth, Te, heavenly power that comes from harmony, and fifth, Wen, the arts of peace.

The training ground for the acquisition of these virtues is the constellation of relationships which revolve around Hsiao. The cornerstone of goodness, Hsiao is given naturally. Because humanity owes its existence to parents, respect for them grows naturally. When people love their parents and serve them gratefully, their moral sense is born. Following this is the relationship of husband and wife, elder and younger sibling, elder and younger friend, ruler and subject.

Education through these relationships creates ideal character for both leaders and the population at large. Confucius was most concerned about leadership and proper governing. Once, when asked by a powerful ruler for wisdom and advice about how he could better rule the subjects of his province, Confucius quietly replied that the emperor should first learn to rule himself. In *The Great Learning*, Confucian political philosophy is expounded in terms of three principles and eight general rules. The principles are: to manifest illustrious virtue; to show love for people; and to rest in the highest good. The rules are: to investigate many things; to extend knowledge; to be guided by sincere thoughts; to "rectify" your heart; to cultivate personality; to regulate your own family; to govern your state well; and to bring peace to the world.

Confucius, who never considered himself as anything more than a transmitter of "the ancients," came to the end of his life with virtually no external trappings of having greatness. Lao Tzu's external legacy was even less. The latter never even attempted to create a following, and is said to have reluctantly written the *Tao Te Ching* in a day or two at the request of a 'gatekeeper' at a westerly mountain pass. Inconceivably, the influences of these two teachers (themselves like Yang and Yin) brought the China of their day (and in centuries to come) out of the horror, brutality and inhumanity of the plummeting Chou Dynasty, an age of war without chivalry and unthinkable social disintegration.

Conclusion

In this cursory overview of the birth of these great traditions one clearly sees the opening up of heaven over the known world in the 6th century BC. Each aspect of human transformation, from the profoundly metaphysical and transcendent in the Upanishads, to the social reflection of the ideal of heaven in Confucius, appear. God, human responsibility and social relations reflecting the ideal were taught at once. These teachings reversed the dark age and began to create civilizations which can respond well to the teaching of the true parents when they seek to order life and society according to God's original ideal.

17 | JESUS AND CHRISTIANITY

INTRODUCTION

At the culmination of four centuries of intense global preparation for true parents, Jesus was born in Bethlehem, Israel. Despite his all-important mission, his parents were poor and he started life in very humble circumstances. During his 33 years on earth he reached some prominence as a radical religious reformer and worker of miracles but he was not known well beyond a limited circle of relatives and disciples. Nevertheless, his short life shook the world. Today there are more followers of Jesus than any other religious figure in history. Clearly his life was of great importance in the providence of restoration.

To understand Jesus from the point of view of providential history, one must examine his life in the context of his identity and mission in the dispensation of restoration. Getting a clear picture of Jesus is not easy, primarily because the four gospels that record his words and deeds are inadequate at best, each account somewhat different from the others and all of them brief. If the recorded words of Jesus were separated from the stories of his life and placed in a book of their own, it would be a slim volume indeed. Further compounding the problem, the dearth of reliable contemporary biographical material on Jesus as a historical figure has resulted in the creation of many popular myths regarding who he was and what he did. These can present obstacles to understanding Jesus in a true historical and providential context.

His public mission lasted for less than three years, at the end of which he was rejected by the very people he had come to save, whose leaders handed him over to the Roman governor for execution. Why did this happen? How was it that the descendants of Jacob, who had been preparing for a savior for 2000 years, allowed the death of the very person they had awaited with such longing? This chapter discusses the identity and mission of Jesus, why that mission could not be completed and what the consequences of this were for the providence of restoration.

The Mission of Jesus

Ever since Adam and Eve fell, God's central objective in history has been the restoration of the position of first ancestors, sinless true parents who could fulfill the three blessings. Only through true parents can sinful human beings be separated from the lineage of their false parents, Adam and Eve, and 'reborn' into the lineage of God's true love. All the efforts of God's central figures in the providence until Jesus, that is the work of the prophets, saints and sages of the Old Testament era, had been directed towards laying a foundation for true parents. Jesus came to reap the harvest of those efforts and to complete the three blessings. He was to save fallen humanity by offering people a way to leave Satan's dominion and enter the realm of God's dominion through 'grafting' onto the lineage of true parents.

On the basis of the individual and family foundations for true parents created by four generations of Abraham's family, and the tribal and national foundations laid by Moses and Joshua, Jesus was sent by God to restore the position of Adam. Once victorious as a second Adam on the individual level he would choose a wife to restore Eve and together they would become true parents. Their offspring would be true children and the starting point of a sinless lineage. All who united with the true parents and their descendants would be grafted into that pure lineage and separated from the dominion of Satan. In this way the Kingdom of Heaven would be established on earth.

This mission could not be accomplished unless those prepared to receive Jesus did indeed welcome and follow him. They would have to allow him to educate them in an understanding of God's providence so that they could fully understand and support him in his mission. However, Jesus was rejected by the Israelites and crucified because they did not recognize him as the messiah. His words and deeds contradicted their expectations for the messiah, leading to doubts about his authenticity.

Having labored for 2000 years to raise the mentality, spirituality and responsibility of the Children of Israel so that they could fulfill their providential role, and having often been bitterly disappointed by their faithlessness, God had good reason to be concerned about how the Israelites would respond to Jesus. For this reason, many conditions were laid to prepare them to receive Jesus. In the final stages of this process conditions were laid for the people of Jesus' time to accept him as the messiah. The pattern of indemnity resembled Moses' three courses to lay a national foundation. In the life of Jesus there were three attempts made to set up a world-wide foundation for true parents. The conditions for restoration moved from the national to the world-wide level on the foundation laid by Moses and Jacob and because Jesus' mission was to save all humankind. An examination of the three providential courses in the life of Jesus reveals why he was rejected by the Israelites despite the great efforts God had made to prepare them.

The First World-wide Course

Jesus came to be a true father for humankind. He came to be a true parent, not to prepare the way for true parents. The man sent to complete the world-wide foundation for true parents was John the Baptist. The son of Zacharia, High Priest of Israel, John was a man of great faith who lived an ascetic life in the desert. He preached a powerful message of repentance and baptized followers to purify them of their sins in readiness for the coming messiah. Through living a life of rigorous discipline and obedience to the law, John succeeded in laying a foundation of faith, and by winning the devotion of followers through his preaching and baptizing he made a foundation of substance with the Israelites.

John's foundation was established for the messiah and therefore had to be offered to Jesus. It was not for John to use for his own promotion in Israel. However, John doubted the messiahship of

Jesus and held back from offering himself and his followers to Jesus. John expected the messiah to come in glory and demonstrate superhuman attributes. He also expected Elijah to return to Israel in a miraculous manner to announce the messiah. These unrealistic expectations, coupled with the problem of accepting his poor cousin as the long-expected savior, caused John's lack of faith in Jesus. If he had truly believed in Jesus, he would naturally have followed him. But despite receiving confirmation about the messianic mission of Jesus, in particular through the miraculous public anointing of Jesus by the holy spirit of God, John continued to question Jesus and went his own way instead of becoming a disciple of Christ.

The mission of John was particularly critical to Jesus because John fulfilled a very important prophecy of Malachi. As the last prophecy of the Old Testament Age, given 400 years before Jesus, it said Elijah would return to Israel to prepare the way for the messiah. Elijah was a prophet who had, according to the Bible, been taken to Heaven in a chariot of fire at the end of his life, rather than facing normal death. Many Jews expected Malachi's prophecy to be fulfilled through a dramatic return of Elijah. Thus if Jesus was the messiah, they wanted to know where the promised Elijah was. When Jesus was asked this question by his own disciples he indicated that John the Baptist had come in the place of Elijah. However, when asked about this, John denied being Elijah.

By this denial, John put Jesus in an extremely difficult position regarding the Israelites. It was much easier for them to believe John, who came from a credible and respected religious background, than to believe Jesus, who was raised in the home of Joseph, a poor carpenter. Without the help of John, Jesus could not penetrate the leadership echelons of Israel but instead had to work with simple folk who accepted him at their own level of understanding but were poorly equipped to introduce him to the rest of the nation. To accomplish his mission Jesus had to convince the Israelites of his identity and purpose. With the loss of John the Baptist as the foundation-builder for his mission in Israel and his bridge to the people, Jesus was faced with the overwhelmingly difficult task of convincing the Israelites of his messiahship by himself.

The first world-wide course to set up a foundation for true parents ended in failure because John the Baptist did not offer his own foundation and support to Jesus.

The Second World-wide Course

When John the Baptist failed his mission, Jesus set out to restore John's lost foundation by laying a foundation himself. In effect, he determined to make indemnity conditions to prepare for his own messianic mission. He did this by going to the desert to fast for 40 days. At the end of the fast he was tempted three times by Satan. These temptations aimed at getting Jesus to give up his mission of restoring the three blessings, but Jesus overcame them. This success set up a foundation of faith for the second course.

To lay a foundation of substance, Jesus had to win the people's love and obedience. Yet the Israelites did not understand him. Even his 12 closest disciples only partially grasped his mission, being simple men of faith with little education or ability in spiritual matters. People were attracted to Jesus mainly because of his healing powers and the miracles he performed, rather than the words of truth he uttered. But the only reason he performed remarkable feats was to help them recognize him as the messiah. In the end, despite his great efforts, Jesus could not win the hearts and minds of the Israelites.

When Jesus saw that his mission to set up a foundation of substance was not succeeding, he began to tell his disciples that he would have to offer his life for the salvation of humankind and that the mission of the messiah would have to be completed in a second coming. As the end drew near, he withdrew to the Garden of Gesthemane to pray for God's guidance. Even at that final, desperate moment, as soldiers approached to apprehend him, his three closest disciples slept. They simply did not realize his importance and the gravity of the situation.

When Jesus was arrested and taken for trial before the religious authorities of Israel, his disciples abandoned him altogether, leaving him to be convicted of heresy and turned over to the Romans for execution. He ended his life on the cross surrounded by enemies and deserted by his followers. Without even his disciples showing loyalty and obedience to him, Jesus was unable to lay a foundation of substance. To reverse the fall, where humans died spiritually because of their disobedience to God, individuals must be willing to obey God at the cost of their lives.

As a minimum condition of restoration, the three main disciples of Jesus, Peter, James and John, should have been willing to offer their lives to save Jesus. As the spiritual children of Jesus, the second Adam, they represented Cain, Abel and Seth. By showing complete obedience to the restored Adam figure, they would have made a condition for the restoration of both generations of Adam's family, a minimum foundation of substance to enable Jesus to pursue his global mission. Instead, they slept during his hour of greatest need and scattered when he was captured by soldiers. When Peter, Jesus' most important disciple, was questioned about his relationship with the Nazarene, he denied his discipleship three times.

Jesus' crucifixion marked the end of his efforts to lay a foundation of substance in the second course. Instead of Cain uniting with Abel, the people of Israel turned Jesus over to the Roman governor Pilate for execution. The crucifixion of Jesus repeated Satan's murder of Adam and Cain's assassination of Abel. The second course ended in failure.

The Third World-wide Course

Although Jesus was totally rejected by the people, he never lost faith. On the cross he forgave the Israelites their mistake in killing him, even though he had every reason to feel resentful towards them. In his patience and faith at that moment of ultimate agony and frustration he reversed the loss of faith and anger of Moses at Horeb. Thus, although Satan could attack and destroy the body of Jesus, he was unable to defeat his spirit. In this way Jesus gained a great spiritual victory over Satan, a victory that opened the way for a successful third world-wide course of restoration.

After his death, Jesus engaged in a three-day spiritual battle with Satan. Gaining the victory, he immediately began to minister to his followers, appearing to them repeatedly and encouraging them to believe in him and to carry out the mission he had given them. He told them they should prepare for a second coming of the messiah. Over a 40-day period he built a strong foundation with his followers, after which he left their immediate presence to begin his course in the spirit world. The final departure of his spirit from the presence of his disciples is called the ascension.

Ten days after the ascension, the Holy Spirit descended on a gathering of 120 of his followers, filling them with inspiration and confidence, and empowering them to go out and preach their belief that Jesus was the messiah. It was reported that on that first day of spiritual outpouring some 3000 people converted to belief in Jesus. From that time on his disciples had the strength of conviction to sacrifice themselves for Jesus, a commitment of faith they had lacked before his crucifixion.

In the third course, then, Jesus successfully laid a spiritual foundation of faith through his unwavering faith on the cross, his victory over Satan in the spirit world and the 40-day spiritual ministry to his disciples. He also succeeded in laying a spiritual foundation of substance because his disciples reached a level of devotion where they were willing to die for him. Thus the third course was victorious only on a spiritual level. Instead of establishing the promised Kingdom of Heaven on earth by fulfilling the three blessings, Jesus established a spiritual realm of separation from Satan, accessible to all those who believe in him and follow his teachings and example. Thus Christians can achieve spiritual salvation through living in obedience to God and Jesus.

The Crucifixion Was Not God's Will

It is clear from this explanation of the three world-wide courses that the crucifixion was not the original will of God but rather the result of human failure to obey the will of God. Rejection by the Israelites meant that Jesus was unable to fulfill the three blessings and was forced to go the way of suffering instead. While there were Old Testament prophecies anticipating a suffering course for the messiah, their purpose was to warn of the consequences of faithlessness and not to announce an eventuality. Only after the fact have Christian scholars concluded that prophecies of a suffering messiah were to be fulfilled in the first advent while prophecies of a glorious and victorious messiah would be fulfilled in the second. Old Testament scriptures never speak of the messiah coming twice.

If the crucifixion had been the will of God, one would expect to see Christians, as the sinless inheritors of Jesus' victorious fulfillment of the messiah's mission, embodying the ideal of true men and women and living in an ideal world of peace and prosperity. Yet this is not so. Christians, although benefited by their inheritance from Jesus, are still born under the influence of sin and live in a world that has all the ills that existed before the advent of Jesus.

Jews point to the crucifixion of Jesus as confirmation of their conviction that he was not the messiah. According to most relevant Old Testament prophecies, the messiah was supposed to be a glorious king who would put their enemies to flight and establish the Kingdom of Heaven in Israel. There was no evidence of Jesus having accomplished this in a life that ended on the cross. However, missing in this Jewish viewpoint is recognition of the all-important role of human responsibility. God always works according to His own principles, whereby His will is realized only when human beings fulfill their own responsibility in responding to God. Thus, as for all other central figures, the messiah's mission can only be successfully completed through the willing cooperation of those chosen to receive and follow him.

Muslims believe it was not Jesus himself who was crucified but someone resembling him who was executed in his place. While the Principle confirms that the spirit of Jesus was indeed victorious and undefeated by the crucifixion, Jesus offered his own body as a condition of indemnity for the salvation of humankind. In fact it was this offering that laid the foundation for the success of the third world-wide course of restoration, which was a spiritual victory and the basis for the Christian providence.

Christology

In Jesus the three great monotheistic religions both meet and diverge. His identity and mission are debated endlessly among believers of the three faiths because of the differences in their understanding of him. For Jews, Jesus was not the awaited messiah but one of their own who broke with tradition and founded his own religion. For Christians he was the messiah and savior who carried out his God-given mission by dying on the cross. Some Christians believe he was God incarnate, the member of a mystical trinity with God and the Holy Spirit. Yet others believe he was a man with divine attributes. Muslims believe that he was a great prophet who helped pave the way for Mohammed.

According to the Principle, Jesus was a man, not God. There is only one God and Jesus came to restore humanity's relationship with God. Jesus was chosen as a second Adam by God to accomplish a historic mission for which his lineage prepared him. He was born to parents whose ancestors had made special conditions to purify their descendants and protect them from the dominion of Satan. These conditions made it possible for Jesus to be born free from sin. His purity uniquely qualified him for his messianic mission.

But he was a man. He became thirsty and hungry, tired and angry, and he prayed to God for help. He had to struggle with all the things any ordinary person must struggle with, but his sinless nature set him apart from fallen men, enabling him to live a morally perfect life. Since his mission was to restore the mistakes of Adam, he had to be a man like Adam. Before the fall cut off his spiritual senses, Adam had the attributes of a true man created in the image of God and capable of understanding and communicating with his Heavenly Father. A person who manifests God's image can have a perfect love relationship with God, like the relationship between a child and the parent it resembles. In this metaphorical sense Adam was to become a true son of God. His descendants would be born out of his physical lineage but internally they would belong to the lineage of God. Jesus was endowed with qualities of character similar to those of Adam before the fall, which enabled him to have a profound relationship with God. In this sense, Jesus was a true son of God.

Trinity and Rebirth

Jesus came as a second Adam to be a true son, brother, husband and father. To fulfill this destiny he needed to find a bride who could unite with him in fulfilling the three blessings. Hence in the Bible he is referred to as a bridegroom. Since the foundation for true parents was not established for him before his crucifixion, he could not complete the restoration of Adam during his lifetime. Therefore, after his spiritual victory in the third course, the Holy Spirit, a feminine manifestation of God, joined him in the position of a spiritual Eve. The Holy Spirit functions as a mother to comfort fallen humans and move their hearts to accept Jesus.

Early church fathers tried to understand the relationship between God, Jesus and the Holy Spirit. This effort led to the promulgation of theories of the Trinity. While traditional Christian theologies hold various views of the Trinity, with the resulting dissension having caused much intra-Christian disputation and bloodshed, the Principle explanation is simple. The trinity of God, Jesus and the Holy Spirit is a spiritual restoration of the original trinity of God, Adam and Eve. Since Jesus did not fulfill the three blessings while on earth, he did so conditionally after his physical death and spiritual resurrection. The Trinity represents the second blessing on the spiritual plane, with Jesus in the Adam position and the Holy Spirit in the Eve position, centered on God.

Since all fallen men and women are born into the lineage of fallen Adam and Eve, they must be reborn into the lineage of true parents. (There is no birth or rebirth without parents.) Jesus could not set up a restored lineage during his lifetime but through his spiritual victory he has been able to offer spiritual rebirth to Christians who follow him and the Holy Spirit. Many devout Christians testify to experiencing spiritual rebirth through Jesus and the Holy Spirit. They receive new life from their spiritual parents.

But the mission of true parents has yet to be accomplished substantially. The failures of Adam and Eve must be reversed completely and a new, God-centered lineage must be established on earth. From this sinless lineage the Kingdom of Heaven will grow to encompass the world. There is no alternative way of salvation.

Christianity

The crucifixion of Jesus meant that he was unable to fulfill prophecy and establish the Kingdom of Heaven. Instead he became the spiritual parent of Christians and the founder of a new religion. In the 2000 years since Jesus walked the earth, Satan has continued his dominion over humanity, bringing untold misery and suffering to billions. The work of restoration will only be completed once the dominion of Satan is broken for good and God can rule His children in an ideal world of true love.

Because the founder of Christianity was killed, the believers who have followed in his footsteps have had to suffer adversity, and many have paid for their faith with their lives. Since Jesus did not establish a victorious foundation on earth, many Christians are other-worldly in their orientation, certain that an ideal world can only be realized in spirit and that the physical world and its evil will have to be literally destroyed in a final judgement of God. The danger inherent in this attitude is a tendency to eschew one's responsibility in the expectation that God will act to end evil. The Principle shows that restoration can only be accomplished through individuals fulfilling their portion of responsibility.

Despite its other-worldly tendencies, Christianity has made indispensible contributions to the advancement of humankind, providing the basis for morality and ethics in Western society and many other parts of the world. It has introduced a new level of human spirituality to the world, producing many internal benefits for humankind, enriching devotional practice, theology and philosophy. Christian idealism has inspired artists and writers, scientists and social reformers, and Christian history is rich in good works performed by men and women committed to obey the teachings of Jesus.

Lessons from Jesus' Course

First, it is not easy for fallen people to recognize God's central figures, even the messiah. Jesus had unique internal qualities and an all-important mission, but to the eyes of his fellow Hebrews he was just another man. A true man is not a superman, but someone who is pure and at one with God. The Israelites had been prepared by God to receive a messiah for 2000 years, but when he finally came they could not recognize him. They never imagined they might not be able to identify the messiah easily when he came, assuming that he would be clearly distinguished from all other people. But their expectations, based on prophecies and their understanding of God's work in the past, were not realistic. Even John the Baptist, who was specially sent by God to introduce Jesus to the people of Israel, was blinded by his own misconceptions about the messiah and how he would save Israel. The failure of the Jewish people to recognize Jesus as the messiah is a caution for all who want to know God's central figures for their time.

Second, one must have a humble attitude in order to recognize a central figure of God. At the time of Jesus, the arrogant Jewish leaders were blind to his virtue and truth whereas a few humble souls could recognize his unique goodness. These humble disciples saw in his actions the works of a true man, and in his words the fulfillment of scriptures. The same test of humility and heart will apply at the advent of true parents, when once again only those who are truly meek and objective before God will be able to recognize him. It is dangerous to be arrogant about one's own spiritual ability and over-confident about one's interpretation of prophecy. Spiritual arrogance, like that of Israel's religious leaders, blinds a person to the invisible work of God.

Third, believers cannot depend solely on the viewpoint of their leaders in judging the veracity of a new providential figure. The leaders of Israel, secular and ecclesiastic, did not accept Jesus. Therefore, to follow them meant to stand in opposition to God's will. Because each person is individually responsible before God for his own ultimate destiny it is vital to augment investigation of truth with intense prayer and soul-searching. This spiritual discipline trains the individual to respond to the dictates of original mind, which is always in harmony with God's will.

Fourth, God does not impose His will on humankind, even through the messiah. Jesus had all the qualifications of a true man and the complete support of God, and yet God did not force the Israelites to accept him as the messiah. Because Jesus was rejected,

God's will was frustrated and God began to prepare again for the coming of true parents. Even when that takes place, the same principle of human responsibility will apply and only if people accept and follow the new Adam and Eve will God be able to accomplish His purpose at that time. Therefore it is not enough to wait for God to act and solve humanity's problems. Individuals must seek out God's will and from their own impassioned search find the central figure who can guide them to God.

Fifth, following a true person is not easy. John the Baptist and the twelve disciples were the best Jesus could find in Israel, but none of them was ready to offer his life for Jesus. The three chief disciples were not even able to remain awake when Jesus needed them the most. To follow Jesus meant to face one's own fallen nature and struggle to overcome it. A disciple of true parents cannot afford to be lazy or lax with matters of constant personal assessment.

Sixth, if Cain fails his mission Abel must take responsibility to complete it. When John the Baptist failed to offer his foundation to Jesus, he made it necessary for Jesus to take over his mission. Although Jesus was sent to humankind as the messiah, in practice he spent the bulk of his public mission in preparing the people to receive the messiah, a task that John was to have done for him. If Jesus had not accepted the responsibility of John, he would not have been able to lay any sort of foundation at all. In their lives of faith, men and women who seek to help God may well have to take responsibility for others who fail in their missions.

Seventh, the fruit of conditions laid on earth can be harvested in the spiritual world. Although Jesus went to the cross a lonely and rejected figure, his unwavering faith through all his trials and tribulations on earth made a foundation for his spiritual victory over Satan. That victory gave him the power to work in the spirit world to save people through the Christian dispensation.

Eighth, messiahship is true parenthood. If the mission of the messiah could be accomplished by an individual working alone in perfect oneness with God, Jesus would have completed the mission by living a morally perfect life. However, history proves that the mission of the messiah could not be completed by Jesus because the Kingdom of Heaven, to be ushered in by the messiah, was not established by him. If it had been, it would exist today.

The messianic mission can only be completed by true parents who establish a sinless lineage as the beginning point of the Kingdom of Heaven on earth.

Conclusion

The life of Jesus provided fallen humanity a glimpse of God's ideal. More than anyone before him, Jesus as the messiah understood the Heart of God and God's desperate urgency to restore His fallen children. He shared this heart with others, but he was not understood and ended his life in loneliness and a tragic death. The purity of his character and the veracity of the words he spoke have been confirmed by history and the hundreds of millions of people that try to follow him today. The ideal world he described and worked to establish in a hostile environment was not realized, but it was brought an important step closer by his life's endeavor and his sacrificial death.

This ideal world will be ushered in by true parents and, therefore, the providence of restoration since the time of Jesus has focused on laying foundations for them on a world-wide level. Christianity has had the central responsibility in carrying out this task, joined six centuries after Jesus by Islam. Since Jews, Christians and Muslims are part of the Abrahamic foundation for true parents, they all continue to have important roles in the mainstream of God's providence of restoration.

The following chapter will show how the principles of restoration produced a pattern of salvation in the two millennia of Christian history that parallels the providence during the 2000 years from Abraham to Jesus. These close parallels confirm that Christianity has played the pivotal role in preparations made for true parents since Jesus lived on earth.

18 PARALLELS IN HISTORY

INTRODUCTION

Although Jesus was unable to complete the messiah's mission, his spiritual victory over Satan paved the way for the providence to move to a new level. Those who accepted and believed in Jesus, the Christians, inherited his victory and assumed the special mission of leading the restoration providence. Once the leaders of Israel had rejected Jesus as the messiah, the primary responsibility for laying a foundation for true parents was transferred from the physical descendants of Jacob to the spiritual lineage of Jesus.

The mission of Christianity has been to restore the 2000 years of Israel's preparation for true parents by indemnifying all the mistakes in the earlier providence. Because of Christianity's central providential role, its history is of particular importance for all humankind. Christians have had the advantage of building on the conditions laid by the Israelites as well as the spiritual foundation established by Jesus. Nevertheless, they have faced many of the same problems as those confronted by the Jews in the earlier dispensation. As this chapter will show, Christian history has followed a course remarkably similar to Israel's. However, instead of significantly shortening the time required to lay a foundation for true parents, Christianity has paralleled Israel's pattern of achieving a few spiritual victories against a background of many providential mistakes. The ultimate consequence has been a 2000-year prolongation of the providence of restoration, with the six main periods of Israel's history mirrored almost perfectly in Christian history. These repeated patterns in the restoration providence produce the *parallels in history* that this chapter examines in the limited context of Israel–Christian history.

A significant difference between the histories of Israel and Christianity lies in the difference between their missions: Israel's was national preparation for the true parents and Christianity's global. Furthermore, those who accepted Jesus and obeyed his words had the benefit of living lives centered on a true son of God whose depth of heart and spiritual understanding were unequalled.

Much of the history of Israel is contained in the Bible, but there is no corresponding scriptural account of the Christian era. The Bible closes with the highly symbolic revelation of John, which follows a sketchy account of the early Christians and several pastoral letters written by early Christian leaders, in particular Paul. But God has been working for the restoration of fallen humans over the past 2000 years with as much determination as He did during the 2000 years before Jesus. The signs of His providence are there to be discovered in the history of the last two millennia.

Undoubtedly the two most important providential developments of this period have been the emergence of Christianity and Islam as the world's most powerful religions. Clearly the phenomenal growth of these two global belief systems is related to God's providence of salvation. This chapter examines the most significant dispensational developments in Christian history, as they parallel the history of Israel, while the following chapter discusses the role of Mohammed and Islam in God's providence.

400 Years of Slavery and Persecution

The 400 years of Hebrew slavery in Egypt were paralleled by 400 years of Christian persecution under the Roman Empire.

Because Jesus, the founder of Christianity, walked a course of suffering and persecution, culminating in his death on the cross, those who have followed in his footsteps have likewise had to go a way of suffering. Many of his early followers were martyred by secular powers, sometimes acting hand in hand with ecclesiastic authorities who persecuted the new religion. In particular, the

Roman Empire, of which Israel/Palestine was a province, opposed the new faith and put many Christians to death, often in extremely cruel ways. The established religions in Israel and Rome felt threatened by the vibrant new faith and did everything possible to crush it. But the persecution did not succeed in destroying Christianity. On the contrary, it flourished. In 325 Emperor Constantine of Rome had a vision of Christ's cross and converted to Christianity. He moved his capital to Byzantium, later Constantinople, where, by the end of that century, Christianity was made the state religion by Emperor Theodosius II.

The 400 years of Christian suffering under Rome paralleled the 400 years of slavery the Israelites underwent in Egypt, where they were under the heel of harsh secular authorities supported by a pagan priesthood. In both cases, the oppressed maintained their beliefs and traditions and, with God's help, eventually triumphed over their oppressors.

400 Years of Judges and Patriarchs

The 400 years of Judges ruling Israel was paralleled by 400 years of church patriarchs ruling the Christian world.

Israel's suffering in Egypt came to an end when Moses was sent to liberate the Hebrew slaves and take them into the promised land of Canaan. Once they reached Canaan, they embarked on a 400-year period of Judges, beginning with Joshua and ending with Samuel. In Canaan they were no longer oppressed slaves but rulers over the land, and for the first time in their history they were able to shape their national destiny. But they made many mistakes, in particular through their failure to set up a clear internal separation between their life of faith centered on God and the idolatry of the Canaanites. Thus instead of establishing a God-centered nation that could receive true parents, they mixed their religion and culture with those of the Canaanites, diminishing the purity of their faith and lineage and losing sight of their central mission.

The second 400 years of Christian history were characterized by deepening divisions within the church and the growing power of church patriarchs, each with his own area of ecclesiastic influence.

The five patriarchal sees were Jerusalem, Alexandria, Antioch, Constantinople and Rome. The patriarchs had considerable power over secular affairs as well as religious, thus enjoying a status similar to that of Israel's judges.

As the power of the patriarchs grew they tended to see each other as rivals rather than brothers in Christ. This trend was coupled with theological ossification as churches drew lines around their beliefs and became increasingly critical of others' theologies. In the midst of this growing competitiveness and power-seeking among the churches, the central mission of Christianity was forgotten. The purpose of the church was to create a foundation for true parents and the Kingdom of Heaven they were to usher in. This required faith and purity, which were somehow overlooked in the rush for external values. Towards the beginning of this period Augustine articulated a vision of a kingdom under God, but the church was not sufficiently pure and focused to implement it.

120 Years of United Kingdoms

The 120 years of the United Kingdom of Israel were paralleled by 120 years of the United Christian Kingdom.

At the end of 400 years of Judges, the last judge, Samuel, responded to the wishes of his people by anointing Saul the first king of Israel. Saul's mission was to unify the 12 tribes of Israel in one kingdom, centered on a temple and the law of Moses. This United Kingdom of Israel was to prepare for true parents, who would make Israel into the cornerstone of the Kingdom of Heaven. But Saul was weak and failed in this mission. His successor, David, was not allowed by God to build a temple. David's son, Solomon, failed to unite the Israelites around the temple he built so that on his death Israel was divided into northern and southern kingdoms, ruled by his servant and son, respectively. Saul, David and Solomon each ruled for 40 years, giving the United Kingdom a life span of 120 years.

Among the leaders of the Christian church, the patriarch of Rome, or Pope, claimed a central position as the man who had inherited the mantle of Jesus' leading disciple, Peter. But this position was not recognized by the other churches, leading to conflicts between the church of Rome in the West and the Eastern Orthodox churches. This schism eventually developed into a complete break between the Eastern and western churches, in 1054.

The relative unity of western Christianity, centered on the Pope (in contrast to the four largely independent sees in the East), provided an opportunity for God to set up a unified Christian nation to prepare for true parents. Therefore, the central providential course within Christianity was focused on developments in the western church.

In the year 800, Pope Leo III anointed Charlemagne first ruler of the United Christian Kingdom. His mandate was to realize Augustine's vision of a "City of God" by creating a united Christendom. Charlemagne was inspired by the ideal of Christian unity under God and proposed union with the Eastern Orthodox churches. Also, with unusual farsightedness, he recognized the importance of good relations between Christianity and the new religion of Islam and made overtures to its leadership in Baghdad. But the dream was not to be fulfilled. Disunity crept into the Christian kingdom and, in the third generation of his family, just 120 years after the anointing of Charlemagne, his grandsons divided the kingdom into three domains, which eventually formed two blocs: the East Franks and West Franks. The faithlessness and disunity of the Christians prevented them from setting up a God-centered kingdom to receive true parents.

400 Years of Divided Kingdoms

The 400 years of the divided kingdoms of Israel and Judah were paralleled by 400 years of division between the eastern and western Frankish kingdoms.

The northern kingdom of Israel did not accept the warnings of the prophets and refused to repent and it was eventually destroyed by the Assyrians. Later, four centuries after the division of Solomon's Israel, the kingdom of Judah in the south, which also refused to obey God and persisted in idolatry, was invaded by Babylon. Jerusalem and the Temple were destroyed and the

Israelites taken into captivity. Thus the 400 years of the divided kingdom came to an end.

In the Christian providence, the division of the United Christian Kingdom into West and East Franks marked the beginning of a long period of division and decline, with only isolated mystics and monastics, such as Francis of Assisi and Dominic, setting the example of true devotion to God. These Christian saints were like the Hebrew prophets who reminded the Israelites of their true purpose and exhorted them to turn from evil ways.

However, instead of laying foundations for the Kingdom of Heaven, Christian leaders were occupied with ecclesiastic conflicts and dragged the church into a quagmire of disputation and disunity. The western church came to see the eastern church and the new religion of Islam as its chief enemies instead of potential allies in the battle against evil. The popes in Rome encouraged Christians in the West to take up arms in crusades to liberate Jerusalem from the "infidel" Muslims. On the way to Jerusalem, the knights took time to attack savagely and destroy communities of Jews and to strike at the heart of Orthodoxy by capturing Constantinople and defiling Saint Sophia, the most important church in the Orthodox world. This lamentable behavior of the western Church could only lead to its isolation from God and invasion by Satan, resulting in spiritual corruption and decline.

210 Years of Exile and Return

The 70 years of Jewish exile in Babylon, followed by 140 years during which the Israelites returned to Jerusalem and restored the Temple, were paralleled by 70 years of papal exile in Avignon and 140 years of disputes before the papacy was fully reinstated in Rome.

When, after repeated warnings, Judah failed to honor God, it's people were taken into captivity in Babylon for 70 years. During their exile, the Israelites repented for their sins in order to be forgiven and allowed to return to Jerusalem. They were chastened by this humbling experience in Babylon and they resolved to rectify their wrongdoing. This repentant attitude made it possible for God to restore them to freedom and allow them to return to their homeland. On returning to Israel they rebuilt Jerusalem and the Temple and recommitted themselves to God. They then embarked on a final 400-year period of preparation for true parents.

In Christian history, when the Crusades ultimately ended in failure, after costing Europe many lives and a great deal of money, the credibility of the papacy came into question. Christians wondered how supposedly infallible popes could have set Christendom on such a disastrous course. The authority of the papacy declined and eventually it was subjected to the indignity of exile under the aegis of Frankish kings, who sought to use it for their own interests. In 1309 King Philip IV arranged for the election of Pope Clement V who moved the papacy to the French city of Avignon, where for 70 years it remained a virtual hostage of the French monarchy. Even secular historians have dubbed this period the Babylonian exile of the Pope because it paralleled Israel's history so closely.

The exile in Avignon marked the nadir of papal authority and prestige. The papacy fell into disrepute because of gross immorality, including the keeping of mistresses, fathering of illegitimate children and other abuses. Religious authorities who were supposed to represent Abel were completely dominated by political powers who represented Cain. In this disgraceful state, the church could not serve God. After the exile in Avignon ended, there was a further period of confusion and disunity in the papacy, with three popes vying for universal recognition at one point. The papacy was eventually confirmed in Rome once more, but without the church having undergone the self-purification it desperately needed.

400 Years of Final Preparation for True Parents

The 400 years of global preparation for true parents that preceded the arrival of Jesus were paralleled by a second 400-year period of global preparation for true parents, initiated by renewal of the Christian church.

As in the history of Israel, revitalization of the church came from reformers who were dismayed by what they saw in their religion, including corruption of the leadership, and spoke out forcefully against it. In Israel's history, the reformers were, generally, the prophets, who urged believers to repent of their evil ways and return to the true religion, and who warned of the dire consequences of failing to change. In Christian history, a growing number of lay Christians, empowered by the new culture of learning fostered by the Renaissance, became distrustful of self-serving church dogma and began to study the Bible themselves. Several prominent Christian scholars started to speak out against the Church's violations of scriptural commands and standards. In particular, they attacked its teachings on the status of the Pope and the practice of selling indulgences, neither of which could be defended scripturally.

Several of these critics paid with their lives for speaking out against the church. But in 1517, when Martin Luther nailed his 95 Theses, which included criticism of the practice of papal indulgences, to the church door in Wittenberg, he inadvertently triggered a full-scale revolt against Rome. This Protestant Reformation ended once and for all the monolithic control of Rome over western Christians. It, and the counter-reformation it engendered in Roman Catholicism, initiated a massive purification of the church and inaugurated a 400-year period of final preparation for true parents.

Conclusion

The 2000 years of Christian history have closely paralleled Jewish history and have served to lay a foundation for the realization of God's purpose for humankind, an ideal world of true love. Based on the spiritual victory of Jesus, this foundation is itself spiritual and can only be fully manifested through the coming of true parents. The dispensation of restoration in the Christian era has been prolonged because of the many mistakes made by religious and political leaders chosen to play key roles in the providence of God. Nevertheless, many fine Christian men and women of faith have left a rich legacy of spiritual insight and inspiration.

When it came, the Protestant Reformation was a desperately-needed movement of purification for western Christianity, and it set in motion forces that have transformed the world over the past four centuries. In this period humankind has been prepared for a new Adam and Eve who will complete the work of Jesus and all the prophets and saints of the history of restoration. The final four-century period of global preparation for true parents will be explained in Chapter 20. As a basis for that explanation, the next chapter discusses the life of the prophet Mohammed and the role of Islam in the providence.

19 | MOHAMMED AND ISLAM

INTRODUCTION

During the past 2000 years there have been two major providential developments: first, the birth and global expansion of Christianity, and, second, the advent of Islam and its dramatic growth into the world's second largest religion. At the end of the 20th Century, almost half the world's five billion people are either Christian or Muslim, with Islam growing faster than Christianity. There is a dispensational reason for this spectacular growth of Islam, which will be explained in this chapter.

The Roots of Islam

As discussed in Chapter 12, Ishmael, the elder of Abraham's two sons, could not receive God's blessing when Abraham's position as father of faith was passed to Isaac, the second son. Abraham had made a mistake in the sacrifice of birds and animals but through his determination to restore that mistake he offered his son as a sacrifice. In the original dispensation, Abraham was to lay a foundation of faith after which Ishmael and Isaac would lay a foundation of substance. God's blessing would then have been given to Isaac and Ishmael.

Because Ishmael was not responsible for losing his providential position in Abraham's family, and the blessing that came with it, God's promise to bless him became a commitment to be fulfilled in time. Ishmael, like Jacob, became the father of twelve sons who became the patriarchs of 12 tribes. These 12 tribes, cousins to the 12 tribes of Israel, were progenitors of the Arabs. The Ishmaelites inherited the burden of a blessing denied, which created a historical base for resentment towards the Israelites.

But since the pattern for giving blessings in the providence of restoration is for God to use Abel as His channel to uplift Cain, the primary providential objective for God has been to establish the position of Abel, so that His blessings could be given to all fallen humanity, centered on Abel.

When Jacob, as Abel, was victorious in making a foundation of substance with Esau, the whole of Isaac's family received God's blessing. God chose the descendants of Jacob to expand the foundation for true parents from the individual to national level, because through this lineage they inherited the victorious foundations made in the four generations of Abraham's family.

The true parents, as universal Abel figures, are to share God's blessing with the rest of humankind, including the Ishmaelites. Thus it was the mission of Isaac's lineage to embrace the descendants of Ishmael and to include them in preparations to receive true parents. By participating in the providence in this manner, the Ishmaelites would earn God's blessings and their resentment towards the Children of Israel would dissolve. However, this cooperation did not come about and the relations between Arabs and Jews have remained problematic to this day. Only through true parents giving true love to the offspring of both sons of Abraham can the historic conflict between them be finally resolved.

Because the providence of restoration is always focused on the pivotal mission of laying a foundation for true parents, the central historical path to that objective is where God is most active with humankind. So it was after Abraham's family. Naturally, God gave special love and guidance to the chosen people because through them the whole world was to be restored. Consequently, both the Bible and the Koran focus their attention on the central figures in the lineage of Jacob (Joseph, Moses, Joshua, David, Solomon, etc), up to and including Jesus. This is the lineage that has been discussed in previous chapters of the history of restoration.

Because of the providential importance of Ishmael, there were points along the path of Jacob's descendants where God's concern for Ishmael's lineage is clearly evident in His efforts to bring the two lines of Abraham's family together. For example, when Moses was sent into exile from Egypt, he was protected by an Arab farmer, Jethro, and married his daughter, Zipporah, making a family base for the two sides to join in a common providence. The prolongation in the providence after Moses delayed any progress in the unity between the Jews and Arabs.

Throughout the era of Judges the Abel position was not properly established in distinction from the Cain world of Canaan. When the circumstances were finally right for Israel to stand as the Abel nation, Solomon failed to unite his people with God and the law of Moses, opening the door for Satan to invade Israel and preventing the Israelites from fulfilling Abel's mission. Specifically, Solomon and the Queen of Sheba could have been a couple that brought the two lines of Abraham's family together, but this possibility was rendered moot by the corruption of Solomon's faith.

There were no further opportunities until Jesus himself came as the true father of humankind. In his words and deeds he frequently emphasized that his mission was not just to save the Jews but to save all people. This is the mission of true parents. When he was rejected by the Israelites, he was prevented from fulfilling this mission and could not transmit God's blessings to the Israelites or the Ishmaelites. However, because Jesus himself was victorious over Satan on the cross and successfully completed a spiritual foundation for true parents, Christians were put in the position to inherit the mission of the Israelites.

The first 400 years of the Christian era offered followers of Jesus an opportunity to indemnify the first 4000 years of the providence (Adam to Jesus in scriptural time) and inherit substantially the position of chosen people from the Israelites. A successful first four centuries of Christianity would have completed the formation and growth stages (two 200-year periods) of a Christian condition to restore the foundation for true parents (two 2000-year periods) lost with the crucifixion of Jesus. The third 200-year period of the Christian era would then have been the time for completion of the Christian foundation for true parents, with Christianity pioneering a new level of restoration. In this restoration scenario, the first six centuries of Christian history would have encapsulated all of restoration history, which otherwise was extended to six thousand years (from Adam to the present day, the time of the coming of the true parents).

As shown in the previous chapter, the church did not succeed in establishing a purified foundation for true parents in its first 400 years. Consequently, by the end of the fourth century Christianity could not be confirmed as the global Abel and therefore entered a long history of wandering in the wilderness of the fallen world in a prolonged providence. These shortcomings in Christianity meant that it could not restore the errors of the Israelites and was not able to embrace the Ishmaelites. Thus the stage was set for God to send Mohammed as a prophet to the Ishmaelites.

The Mission of Mohammed

Because neither the physical (Israelite) nor the spiritual (Christian) lineage of Isaac successfully completed conditions to qualify as Abel and lay the foundation for true parents by the sixth century after Jesus, God chose to bless the Ishmaelites directly and set up a providence to complement and counterbalance Christianity by sending the prophet Mohammed to the Arabs. Historically, Islam is the only major prophetic religion to appear since Jesus gave birth to Christianity. This makes Mohammed the last of the Abrahamic prophets.

Mohammed's mission was to purify the lineage of Ishmael, to separate it from idolatry and to provide it with a clear understanding of God's truth so that it could fulfill a providential role in preparing for true parents. In this way, Mohammed would lay a foundation for true parents with Ishmael's descendants, bringing them directly into the orbit of the central providence of restoration.

Mohammed's teaching, inspired by revelations, was a radical critique of the polytheism of his native Mecca and a validation of the Jewish and Christian prophets and scriptures. Among the basic doctrines he introduced to his people, he emphasized monotheism, God's ideal for the creation, human responsibility, the human fall, punishment for sin and an eventual end to the world of evil. He also demythologized Jesus, stressing that he was a man, not God;

and he contradicted the notion that it was God's will that Jesus die on the cross.

Mohammed's teachings formed the core message for believers in Islam, which means total surrender to God. He taught that everyone who so surrendered was a Muslim, with Abraham specifically mentioned as an early Muslim. Through Islam, Mohammed brought unity to the disparate tribes of Ishmael, establishing a civilization that carried God's blessing to the Arabs and all others who adopted the Muslim faith.

Mohammed's mission and teaching also were a judgement on erroneous elements that had crept into Christianity in its first centuries of existence. He directly challenged spurious Christologies, doctrines of the Trinity, worship of icons and other dubious theologies and practices that were created by early Christians in the absence of relevant teachings by Jesus and his disciples. Muslims also challenged Christianity in the realm of religious propagation, spreading rapidly in the Middle East, Asia and Africa, in particular.

The Mission of Islam

Since God is one and His will is one, the mission for all religions is also one. Religions vary because of the differences in the time and place of their founding, but they all exist for a common mission, to lead fallen humanity back to God. Since fallen nature can only be removed completely through true parents, all religions work to prepare humanity to receive true parents. Because of common ancestral roots, Islam, on the one hand, and Judeo-Christianity, on the other, share parallel, fraternal missions. They should cooperate like two brothers working together to prepare the way for true parents.

In any family there are differences between the children. When harmonized, these differences are what make a family delightful and enriching. The differences between Christianity and Islam reflect differences in their backgrounds and providential roles. They should cooperate harmoniously for the common purpose of God. Unfortunately, though, the history of their relations has been far from harmonious. All too often they have fought each other instead of working together. For cooperative relations to prevail, there must be real mutual understanding as to what role each is playing in God's overall providence. With true understanding, differences can be seen as complementary strengths rather than unreconcilable contradictions.

Mohammed and the Koran

Mohammed was born in 570 and spent the first 40 years of his life preparing for his prophetic mission. Surrounded by the idolatrous people of Mecca, in western Arabia, he sought the truth of God, which was revealed to him by the angel Gabriel. The revelations he received were presented to him as the culmination of the prophetic tradition reaching all the way back to Adam. They accepted the revelations of previous prophets and then added a body of instruction covering major theological issues and spelling out clear guidelines for a life of faith.

These revelations were given to Mohammed over a 21-year course, beginning in 610. The first 12 years he spent in Mecca under most adverse conditions because the Meccans persecuted him and his followers severely, forcing several to flee into exile in Abyssinia on two separate occasions. Several times Mohammed was driven to the brink of despair, but he never gave up his mission and eventually his real worth was recognized by tribes of nearby Yathrib. Seventy elders from Yathrib invited Mohammed to assume leadership over their town, to resolve tribal disputes and establish order among their people.

In 622 Mohammed and his followers emigrated from Mecca to Yathrib. In many respects the move was an escape from confinement, and the prophet himself had to hide in a cave for three days while angry Meccans sought him out. The liberation and emigration of the early Muslims was similar to the liberation of the Israelites from Egypt, also accomplished after three days of separation from their enemies. Because of its significance to Muslims, the Islamic lunar calendar takes 622 as its first year. For Muslims it is considered year one hijary (of the emigration).

Once in Yathrib, which was renamed Medina (The City),

Mohammed set about creating a theocratic state according to the revelations he had received in Mecca and continued to receive in Medina. In addition to explaining God's will for humankind, the revelations provided detailed instructions for leading a God-centered life and the fulfillment of human obligations to God and fellow human beings. After Mohammed's death, these revelations were collected in 114 Suras, or chapters, and compiled as the Koran, which means literally the Reading (of Truth).

The Koran adds to the material in Biblical scriptures about many of the figures in the providence of restoration, often providing its own emphasis. It stresses throughout that there is only one God, not many, as the Meccans believed, and makes it very clear that Jesus was a man and not God. It also says that Jesus was victorious over death. It shows that each person is responsible before God for his actions, which is the basis for the law of indemnity. The rewards for living a faithful life are spelled out in appealing terms, while the punishments for disobedience to God are presented in graphic detail.

And Islam provides a believer with a basic five-fold path for the fulfillment of his responsibility: confession of faith in God and Mohammed; prayer five times a day; tithing one fortieth of his wealth; fasting annually throughout the lunar month of Ramadan; and making the pilgrimage to Mecca at least once in his lifetime. These 'five pillars of Islam' have guided hundreds of millions of believers throughout the world in leading faithful lives.

The Expansion of Islam

Mohammed was not only a prophet but also a very successful leader. During his brief decade of leadership in Medina he succeeded in uniting the disputatious tribes of Arabia under the banner of Islam. This national foundation for Islam enabled the new religion to explode out of the Arabian Peninsula after his death (632), and in little more than a century it spread all the way to the borders of France in the West and China in the East. In many parts of the world Islam succeeded in introducing monotheism where Christianity had proved unsuccessful in the same endeavor. One reason for this comparative success was Islam's singular focus on God in contrast to the Christian emphasis on Jesus and a teaching encumbered by a number of hard-to-understand theological concepts.

The dramatic expansion of Islam, from the individual to the family, tribal, national and global levels, demonstrated the pattern of restoration according to the principles of restoration. To establish a global foundation, a national foundation is needed. Thus once Mohammed had united Arabia under Islam, the new religion could move to a world-wide level very rapidly. The Kingdom of Heaven, which is the dominion of true love, will begin with one family and then expand to one clan, one tribe and one nation. From that nation God's domain will expand to the whole world.

The expansion of Islam was marred by an excessive use of force against believers of other faiths. This caused resentments against Muslims that in some cases lingers to this day. Islam was to be disseminated through service and love and not by the force of arms. God is a God of love, not violence and warfare. His representatives must emulate him.

Islam and Christianity

Both Christianity and Islam spread throughout the world, expanding outward from their origins in the Middle East. But the manner in which each expanded varied from the other because of the differences between their founders' courses. Jesus' course resulted in a spiritual victory and therefore the expansion of Christianity was on a spiritual level; the victory of Mohammed was spiritual and physical and therefore the expansion of Islam took place on the spiritual and physical levels. Differences between the two in the spiritual dimension were also reflective of the two men's different missions, Jesus having been sent as the messiah and true parent, Mohammed as a prophet to prepare for the coming of true parents.

Since Christianity and Islam had parallel missions in preparing a foundation for true parents, there should have been a cooperative relationship between them in history. However, because of resentments and misunderstanding on both sides, this was rarely the case. Nevertheless, history reveals God's efforts to get the two brother religions to work together.

When the United Christian Kingdom was established by Charlemagne (800), the United Islamic Empire was at its zenith under the Abbasids. Harun Al Rashid was the Caliph in Baghdad (786–809), overseeing a brilliant flourishing of science and literature in his extensive domain. The two leaders exchanged gifts, but no substantial cooperation was initiated, although there were many good reasons for Christendom, which was dominant north and east of the Mediterranean Sea, and Dar Al Islam, concentrated to the south and east of the Mediterranean, to join hands in developing the world they knew.

However, distrust and enmity dominated and soon the two religions were at each other's throats. The popes in Rome launched a series of crusades against the Muslims, adding to the Christian and Muslim blood already shed during the expansion of Islam. The crusades set the two religions on a collision course that has characterized their relations ever since. Muslims say the Bible contains misrepresentations of God's word, distorted by dishonest Jews and Christians, while Christians see nothing in the Bible to anticipate the coming of Mohammed and consequently reject Islam, characterizing it as an illegitimate perversion of their own faith. Thus continued conflict, based on mutual misunderstanding and suspicion, has soured the relations between Christianity and Islam, greatly hampering God's providence for both religions.

When the United Christian Kingdom failed to lay a foundation for true parents because of disunity, it divided into the kingdoms of the East and West Franks, beginning the 400 years of divided kingdoms. In the history of Islam, the United Islamic Empire of the Abbasids gradually began to fall apart as pieces broke away under leaders who increasingly rejected the supremacy of Baghdad and claimed parts of the Muslim territory as their own. The caliphate fell into serious decline from the mid-10th century and was overtaken by conquering Seljuk Turks in the mid-11th Century. The Turks were in turn conquered two centuries later (1258) by Hulagu's Mongols, who put an end to the Abbasid caliphate.

The caliphate had an important symbolic value in representing continuity of Muslim leadership after Mohammed's death, since the prophet left no male heirs. The first four (orthodox) caliphs to succeed Mohammed, Abu Bakr, Omar, Othman (who compiled the Koran) and Ali, could not set up a lasting and universal tradition because of contentious forces within the Islamic community. An anti-Ali faction wrested the caliphate from him by force, establishing the Umayyad caliphate in Damascus (661), only to have it taken away from them a century later (750) by the Abbasids, whose base was Baghdad. The North African Fatimids claimed the caliphate from Baghdad after they conquered Egypt (969), and eventually, in 1517, the Ottoman Turks moved the caliphate from Cairo to Constantinople when they conquered Egypt. The Caliphate finally died out when the Ottoman Sultanate collapsed and the year-old Republic of Turkey renounced it in 1924.

One result of the internal divisions within Islam was the creation of two main branches, the predominant Sunnis and minority Shias. Sunnis recognize the four orthodox caliphs, whereas the Shias recognize up to an additional eight caliphs or imams (depending on the sect), out of the lineage of Ali, the fourth caliph. For the Shias, Ali holds particular importance as inheritor of Mohammed's central position in the faith and as a model Muslim.

The disunity in Christendom, leading to the decline and eventual exile of the pope, was mirrored in the Islamic world by disunity leading to the decline and virtual demise of the Caliphate. In Christian history, this decline was arrested only once a corrective movement, the Protestant Reformation, took hold after Martin Luther spearheaded efforts to reform the Roman Catholic church in 1517. In Islamic history, decline and disintegration were halted and the Muslim world was reunited under the Ottoman Empire when the Turks conquered Syria, Egypt and the holy cities of Mecca and Medina in 1517, beginning 400 years of Turkish rule. This vast empire extended south from its center in Turkey to encompass the Arab world, west through the length of North Africa and into East and Central Europe, and east into Central Asia. The Ottoman Empire did not parallel the Protestant Reformation as a force for spiritual renewal, but it helped preserve Islam as a unified religio-political power that fostered the spread of monotheism.

By 1517, the Islamic world had reached the threshold of the final 400 years of global preparation for true parents, an era that saw a transformation of the world on all levels and presented Islam with the challenge of fulfilling its providential destiny through full alliance with Christianity in the fight against Satan's dominion.

Lessons from Mohammed's Course

First, God judges and supplements religions until they fulfill their purposes. If Judaism had fulfilled its mission and accepted Jesus, there would have been no need for Christianity. If Christianity had completely incorporated and applied the teachings of Jesus there would have been no need for Islam (the promise to Ishmael would have been fulfilled through the mission of the victorious messiah). God sent Mohammed as a judgement for Jews and Christians after they failed to fulfill God's will, and the revelations in the Koran were given to Mohammed to supplement those in the Bible.

Second, religions vary in content and emphasis depending on their missions. God used Mohammed to bring truth and a way to salvation for many millions of people all over the world, people who without Islam would lack a deep and comprehensive understanding of God and how to be reconciled to Him. Judaism and Christianity are both strongly focused on the messiah and how to receive salvation through him. Islam's focus is more towards the practice of religious obligations for justification before the one true God. Eastern philosophies and religions have their own emphases. The differences in focus translate into differences in culture. Since all religions are inspired by God to prepare humanity to receive true parents and fulfill the three blessings, their diversity offers fallen humans, coming from various cultural backgrounds, many paths to oneness with God. Thus the different religions have different but complementary missions to fulfill within God's global providence of restoration.

Third, Islam established a model for restoration on the prophetic level. By persuading first individuals and families in Mecca, then tribes in Yathrib/Medina, and, finally, the whole nation of Arabia to accept his prophethood and leadership, Mohammed laid a successful foundation for the expansion of Islam to the world-wide level. Through this achievement, Mohammed pioneered a global providence to be perfected on the messianic level by true parents.

Fourth, the prophetic foundation is to prepare believers for the coming of true parents. The Jews inherited the prophetic foundation of the patriarchs in Abraham's lineage up to Malachi to prepare them for Jesus. Muslims inherited the Judaic foundation plus the prophetic foundations of Jesus and Mohammed to prepare them for the true parents to come.

Conclusion

Mohammed was a successful prophet and statesman who in the brief span of 21 years went from persecuted visionary to ruler of Arabia. His success made Islam a powerful tool for the providence and the second largest religion in the world. However, Islam was blessed by God not merely to fulfill His promise to bless Ishmael, but, more importantly, as part of His overall dispensation of restoration. Therefore Islam's mission can only be completed in conjunction with God's work in other religions, especially Judeo-Christianity.

The next chapter will look closely at the 400 years since 1517 to show how these four centuries were the second period of global preparation for true parents, an era in which both Christianity and Islam became world-wide religions exerting unrivaled influence over human affairs, and both were faced with challenges from science and materialism in the final battles to establish God's Kingdom of Heaven on earth.

20 | THE SECOND GLOBAL PREPARATION FOR TRUE PARENTS

INTRODUCTION

The two previous chapters discussed how Christianity and Islam have played leading roles in the providence to prepare the world for true parents in the aftermath of Jesus' crucifixion. Expansion of these two religions was boosted by global developments of providential importance which entered a dramatic period of growth some four centuries ago. The great speed and intensity of these developments was brought about by an acceleration in the providence of restoration as, for the second time, the whole world was made ready to receive the messiah. The preparations this time exceeded by every measure those that preceded the birth of Jesus.

There have been several powerful currents running through this period: religious, philosophical, scientific, economic and political. No field of human knowledge and endeavor is even remotely the same today as it was four centuries ago, when the modern revolution began. The ways people live, travel and communicate have changed so dramatically that today's world would be unrecognizable to the early protestants who were just beginning to taste religious freedom, or to the Ottoman Turks securing control of the Arab heartland.

In the terminology of the 20th Century, the world has become a global village where modern communications and jet travel link all people into a single, world-wide community. The divine purpose behind shrinking physical barriers is to facilitate the unification of the world under one true God. The human race was always intended to be one family, bound together by true love and ordered according to a unified hierarchy of men and women under God and true parents.

This chapter briefly examines some of the major forces that have transformed the world over the past four centuries and how these changes relate to God's providence of restoration.

Religion

The most powerful force in human society is religion. Belief in a supreme being or transcendent spiritual power motivates people to build their lives according to religious principles, whereby they expect to be rewarded for doing good and punished for doing evil. In medieval Europe, the Church of Rome maintained authority over Christian knowledge. Few lay people could read or write and fewer yet knew Latin or Greek, the languages in which copies of the Bible were produced. Without printing presses, there were not many Bibles available anyway. Thus the common folk had to believe whatever the ecclesiastic authorities told them. This made the church responsible for the communication of God's truth to believers, a trust which was frequently abused.

The Protestant Reformation was sparked by criticism of the church from a new class of enlightened laity, men and women who were sufficiently educated to study the scriptures and learn for themselves how the church had grown to abuse its authority. Their revolt against Rome started a snowball of defections from the church, forever changing the face of western Christianity. By the end of the 20th Century there were literally dozens of major Christian denominations and thousands of smaller ones. By and large the rejection of church authority and the proliferation of independent churches made individuals feel more responsible for their own religion. This was a healthy development, leading to enquiry into the meaning of scriptures and the responsibilities of believers.

The Reformation also produced a new Christian zeal, inspiring believers to take the message of Jesus to the four corners of the globe. Missionary movements sprang up to carry the word to nearly all nations, making Christianity a truly global religion for the first time. The Catholic Church had missionized before, but the Reformation stimulated its efforts greatly, especially through movements of the Catholic counter-Reformation. The Society of Jesus, or Jesuits, which was dedicated to spreading the Gospel throughout the world, was one of the most successful Catholic mission organizations. The missionary movement was considerably aided by the development of improved means of international transportation, by land and sea.

Unfortunately, missionary activity was all too often used by those with political and economic interests to secure colonial holdings around the world. Mixing objectives diluted the purity of the Christian outreach and generated resentment towards the Christian powers in the peoples targeted for conversion. Nevertheless, the work of missionaries made God's restoration providence centered on Jesus known to most of the world.

The geographic expansion of Christianity was matched by a growth in theological studies, and all issues were open to question and debate as never before. Numerous schools of theology sprang up, representing a wide spectrum of views. The result was that Christians realized there are many ways of interpreting scriptures, depending on one's position or perspective. Knowing this, Christians have to take personal responsibility for their beliefs. This is positive since it is only when an individual takes responsibility to know and obey God that he can fulfill his God-given purpose.

Islam also spread throughout the world during this period, making major inroads in Africa and Asia. As Islam encountered diverse cultures it proved flexible in adapting to them. During this period spiritual movements were a major source of conversion. Sufi groups, which practiced special rituals aimed at bringing members into direct contact with God and the spirit world, were particularly effective. In the period of final preparation, well-established sects, such as the Qadiriyya, Nakshabandis, Shazlis and Mevlevis, were joined by such groups as the Mahdis of Sudan, the Fulanis of Nigeria and the Sanussis of Libya.

While the Ottoman Empire did not foster a particular movement of religious renewal, it was in many respects tolerant of religious independence and free scholarship. Stimulated by the religious and scientific upheaval in the West, a number of Muslim thinkers began to re-examine their faith critically, in particular seeking to reconcile their beliefs with modern science. Among those of note were Ibn Tamiyah, Mohammed Abdu, Sayyid Amin Ali and Mohammed Iqbal.

Philosophy

When the Protestant Reformation challenged Catholic orthodoxy, a tradition of religious freedom began to take root in western society. Thinkers were liberated to explore with new creativity the basic issues of life: the origin of human beings, their attributes, purpose, potential and destiny. In general, the early Greek philosophers provided the base on which modern philosophers (Kant, Hegel, et al) built their systems. At one point, two important camps emerged out of philosophical debates: the idealists and the materialists. The former sought to construct logically sound theories on principles that recognized the existence of an invisible creator. The materialists did not accept religious belief or speculation about the existence of a transcendent, invisible world in formulating their theories of humanity and the creation. They had great faith in science and its ultimate ability to answer questions about life.

The idealist philosophers provided support for theistic ideologies, whereas the materialists supported humanistic ideologies. The most important materialist thinker was Karl Marx, not because of his brilliant philosophy, profound economic theory or perceptive understanding of history (few of his theories stand up to rigorous scientific questioning), but because his theories provided the ideological basis for the most successful materialistic movement in history: communism. With its denial of God and human spirituality, communism set out to conquer the world for the "workers of the world."

The first communist regime was ushered in by the 1917 Bolshevik revolution in Russia. Like a cancer, atheistic communism spread from Russia throughout the world until by the late 1970s, almost two thirds of the earth came under the control of communist rulers. Only after 70 years of cruel dictatorships and endless lies did the communist monster finally falter and collapse in a heap of unfulfilled promises, leaving behind the corpses of tens of millions of innocent people.

The communists promised a materialistic 'kingdom of heaven', in which "each would receive according to his need and give according to his ability." But despite legitimate concerns about inequities in the fallen world, communists never understood the origin of evil and how it can be defeated. As a result, communism caused much more suffering than it ever mitigated. By denying God, communism was no more than a tool of Satan, a system of false ideals susceptible to his manipulation. Although many sincere people were drawn by its promises and sacrificed to help in the realization of the good world it claimed it could create, they were ultimately deceived and most became disillusioned and deeply disappointed.

Ever since Adam and Eve set up a satanic imitation of the true family, Satan has preceded God in creating false imitations of the ideal world (fallen families precede restored families, fallen tribes, restored tribes, and so on). Communist expansion imitated the pattern of restoration: it began with one individual, Marx, and grew in stages. Once one nation, Russia, was claimed for the new, atheistic faith, it was able to expand rapidly to embrace many states around the world. Thus communism was the perfection of Satan's rule on earth, a world-wide foundation for creating a Kingdom of Hell on earth, a world completely under the dominion of evil.

Today any good library contains many thousands of volumes on philosophy, offering readers a full range of theories on life. Providentially, the purpose of philosophy is to provide a framework for understanding God and true parents in the realm of human reason and logic. However, the plethora of theories is confusing. The important concepts are those that enable men and women to fulfill their God-given purposes in this complex modern world.

Science and Technology

Much of the wisdom of ancient Greece, including the basics of science, was preserved, elaborated and significantly added to by Muslim scholars during the early centuries of the Islamic Empire.

These scholars then transmitted their learning to Europe, especially through Spain and Sicily. This injection of scholarship proved to be a key element in Europe's awakening. The first major scholarly movement in Europe was the Italian Renaissance (which preceded the Protestant Reformation and helped provide critical educational tools to the reformers), followed two centuries later by the Enlightenment.

Both movements were important in stimulating science, which finally began its modern life. Religious authorities agreed to let scientists pursue knowledge of humankind and the universe through postulating theories and gathering empirical data to prove or disprove those theories. Before this, the church held a monopoly on knowledge, judging all ideas by the rules of Christian dogma.

Science, released from the constraints of stifling church authority and erroneous religious doctrines about humans and the universe, gave birth to ever more technologies and thus grew to become the leading force in transforming lifestyles in the modern era. By the end of the 20th Century, science had reached such a pre-eminent place in life that it had supplanted religion as the accepted authority on practically all matters pertaining to human existence. It seemed that science, through the development of appropriate technologies in medicine, communications, travel and the provision of human comforts, could meet all human needs. In many respects this widespread dependence on science signifies the elevation of science to the status of religion, and in today's secularized, science-centered world religious beliefs that cannot meet the criteria of science are suspect. In this reversal of roles between religion and science, people who are afraid to change their materialistic belief systems adhere to scientific theories with dogmatic faith.

However, the world of modern technology, despite all its facilities and benefits, has produced unprecedented human alienation: of individuals from their families, families from their tribes and societies, and groups from their nations. The pervasive alienation of modern society has developed to such an extent that all too many people feel completely alone in the world. Ironically, this is especially the case in crowded cities where the universal preoccupation with survival tends to leave individuals feeling isolated.

God facilitated the development of science as an instrument for the fulfillment of His dispensation, but it was never intended to dominate humanity or take a subject position over religion. Science and technology bring joy to humankind when used in accordance with God's will.

Politics

The last four centuries have witnessed a dramatic change in the way power is wielded and shared. There have been countless upheavals and revolutions, many of them violent, in putting an end to governmental systems that gave absolute power to rulers who abused it at the cost of those they ruled. Although there still are kingdoms, emirates and various forms of dictatorial rule on earth, the idea of democracy has become firmly established as *the* modern way of government, not because it is perfect but because it offers the greatest measure of freedom to individuals in an imperfect world. Democracy allows choice of religion, association and political leadership, and protects other important personal liberties. Ideally, it provides a political environment in which God can work with humans for the development of religion and the creation of a good society.

From God's viewpoint, an ideal system of government would be a theocracy in which political power exists as an expression of God's loving will. Prior to the advent of modern democracy, however, religious institutions failed to preserve the purity they needed to give proper guidance to political leaders. For their part, though, political leaders are to be faulted for frequently acting against the advice of religion or for arrogating religious authority to themselves, damaging religion through abuse of their positions. Thus religion has been harmed by religious and political leaders ignorant of God's will.

Given this experience, democracy has been a relatively better system of government than unrighteous authoritarian rule. Most important, it has protected religious freedom, under which each man and woman can worship God in his or her way, according to personal beliefs. In this way democracy has provided God with an opportunity to educate fallen humans away from primitive or erroneous beliefs and towards true understanding. This is vitally important since the root cause of human error and conflict is ignorance of God's love and truth. However complete a person believes his religion to be, from God's standpoint there is always scope for development and growth in the faith and practice of religion. Until members of the various faiths work together to restore all humankind, religion will not have fulfilled its purpose.

But modern humanity should understand that democracy is not an end in itself. It is not the solution to all human ills. The solution lies in the elimination of evil and the creation of a world of true love, centered on God and true parents. Democracy should be used to foster the development of knowledge that can help individuals realize their deepest aspirations: fulfillment of the three blessings. Thus democracy is only virtuous if it is based on religious values. Once these are removed, it can be abused by satanic influences, including all forms of immorality, and even succumb to totalitarianism of the right (fascism) or the left (communism). Democracy is the best political system devised for the fallen world so far, but in a world of true love such a system would seem archaic and primitive.

Economics

Side by side with political transformation there has been a dramatic change in economies, in how goods and services are made and exchanged. The modern network of sophisticated financial institutions, multinational corporations, individual and multi-owner companies, private and public sector industries, is extremely complex. Karl Marx, who died as recently as 1883, could not have imagined how economies would work a century after he wrote *Das Kapital,* which describes the evils of European capitalism and prescribes the communist remedy.

Political freedom has been accompanied by economic freedom, with each taking turns at leading the other. As a result, at the end of the 20th Century a shrinking percentage of people are the economic property of others and a significant and growing percentage have a range of livelihood choices available to them. This economic freedom is important in enabling individuals to make ideological choices.

The world God created was to provide Adam and Eve with an

abundant life, as long as they fulfilled their role as loving lords over the creation. After they fell they lacked the internal capacity to care for nature properly, leading to a conflict between humans and nature that has persisted to this day. Human destruction of the natural environment out of ignorance and selfishness is now a problem that threatens the survival of all people.

Ideally, prosperity should not be a value in itself but rather the fruit of a good life. In the fallen world, prosperity is often created by one person at the expense of others, thus violating the purpose of the whole which should govern all human affairs. Human greed has caused tremendous suffering in history and continues to do so today.

Essentially, economic power should be used for the benefit of all humankind. God loves all His children and cannot bless a system that deprives some of them of a livelihood while supporting an abundant or even wasteful lifestyle for others. God is fair and just. In a world of true love, that fairness and justice, inherited by His children, will be reflected in an equitable distribution of wealth. For all individuals, the moral way is to use one's wealth for the benefit of others, centered on God's will. The person who does this will find his wealth a blessing. Wealth used selfishly, however, curses its owner, since the creation itself wants to be used for God's will and the betterment of the whole.

The 20th Century

The second 400 years of global preparation for true parents was launched in 1517 and concluded with the end of the First World War and the Bolshevik Revolution in 1917. The four centuries after the Protestant Reformation brought about a world-wide transformation through rapid development in all spheres of human knowledge and endeavor. The early 20th Century saw humanity catapulted into the most incredible era of change in history, with all the developmental trends accelerating at a dramatic pace. There is a providential basis for the rush of events in this century, since this is the time for the coming of true parents and fulfillment of the whole history of humankind. For this reason the 20th Century has witnessed a cosmic final battle between God and Satan. The forces of evil have made a last desperate struggle to dominate the world before the mission of true parents is consummated.

The World Wars

The internal battle between good and evil has produced a century of bloody conflict on an unprecedented scale. In particular, the two world wars and the many conflicts related to the rise of communism as a world-threatening military phenomenon have pitted forces of relative good and evil against each other on a global level. That is not to say that in each conflict there has been a clear separation of good and evil people in opposing camps, but rather that certain leaders have been used by God or Satan to accomplish particular objectives: God has chosen and supported Abel figures to complete a world-wide foundation for true parents; Satan has chosen and supported Cain figures to preserve his dominion over humankind.

In the First World War the Central Powers were in the Cain position. Centered on Germany, Italy and Turkey they fought to maintain and expand their hegemony over other nations. This unrighteous campaign stood in the way of God's providence to liberate nations from imperial domination, freeing them to find their own way to fulfill God's will. The Allies, in the Abel position, were centered on Britain, France and America. They successfully opposed the Central Powers and opened the way for the advance of freedom and democracy throughout the world. However, they made several mistakes in victory. They themselves did not relinquish control of their colonies and they imposed such punitive burdens on the defeated alliance that seeds were sown for the outbreak of a second global conflict.

In the Second World War, the Cain-like Axis Powers, centered on Hitler's Germany, Mussolini's Italy and Imperial Japan, took up arms in unrighteous conquest, killing tens of millions in pursuit of their self-centered ambitions. Again opposed by the Abel-like Allies, centered once more on Britain, France and America, a victory was won for the side of democracy, expanding the liberation of nations world-wide. After their victory, this time the Allies freed their colonies and offered generous terms to the defeated nations, fueling an era of unprecedented prosperity and progress.

The conflict between the Cain-like communist camp, with its ambition to rule the world in the name of atheistic ideology, and the free world can be considered the Third World War. Although the nuclear deterrent apparently prevented outright war between the two sides, the conflict between them frequently produced major wars (Korea, Vietnam, Angola, etc) and resulted in millions of deaths. Only by the end of the 1980s, when communist regimes collapsed in disarray in one country after another, was the global communist threat finally put to rest and the victory of the Abel side unequivocally assured.

Each of these victories for Abel made a condition for the advance of God's providence in the final dispensation. The victory in WWI set up the condition for the birth of true parents; the victory in WWII set up the condition for the launch of the public mission of true parents; and the victory in WWIII opened the way for true parents to complete their mission: fulfillment of the three blessings.

Conclusion

Over the course of the past few centuries, the world has been transformed because of God's intense activity to prepare for the age of true parents. By the end of the 20th Century, Satan's last great attempt to control the world had collapsed with the downfall of communist regimes everywhere. The stage was set, then, for a new era of human well-being in a world of true love. To prepare for that world, religion, philosophy, science, politics and economics have all passed through dramatic changes, and while the world still suffers from human ignorance and evil, the forces of good have been quietly establishing indestructible foundations for the realization of God's will on earth.

The final chapter of this book looks at the phenomena of these last days, foretold in Biblical and Koranic scriptures, and how one can understand the dispensation for true parents in the context of recent developments and the current realities of the world.

21 | THE CONSUMMATION OF HISTORY

INTRODUCTION

The consummation of history is of particular interest to Jews, Christians and Muslims because the Bible and Koran refer extensively to this time, variously called the last days, the judgement day, the end of the world, the day of resurrection, and so on. Most of these eschatological passages depict an end to human life as it has been, a time when God takes drastic action to deal with evil by dividing humanity into two groups: those who are accepted by God and saved from eternal damnation because of their faith and virtue, and those who are judged to be evil and condemned to pay for their sins forever. This final judgement of God is implemented through a series of cataclysmic events that culminate with the saved elevated to Heaven and the damned cast into Hell. The universal desire for Heaven and fear of Hell gives the subject of the last days its power over believers. Understandably, they want to secure their eternal lives by knowing what to expect on the day of judgement.

The purpose of this chapter is to discuss the last days in the light of the principles of creation as well as the principles and history of restoration, which provide an ideological and historical framework for understanding what can be expected at the end of the world and what attitude people should take regarding that time. Without such a framework, any interpretation of scriptures addressing this subject is bound to be highly subjective.

The Principle perspective of history holds that there is a providential purpose behind human events and that all of history is

aimed towards the restoration of true parents through the fulfillment of the three blessings lost by Adam and Eve in the original
creation. The process of restoration follows the principles of
restoration, that is, fallen humans must pay indemnity to lay foundations of faith and substance to make a foundation for true parents. Human beings cannot be restored without fulfilling their responsibility through paying indemnity.

Phenomena of the Last Days

The phenomena of the last days are not exempt from the laws of
restoration. By His own principles, God would not wave a magic
wand to erase evil and separate the good people from the bad because restoration is accomplished by individuals taking responsibility to obey God's words. (If this 'magic solution' was an option for
God, why didn't He use it a very long time ago, avoiding enormous
human suffering?) Only through their own personal fulfillment of
responsibility can people be saved and liberate themselves from
Satan's influence. The events of the last days have to be looked at in
the light of this fact. When Biblical or Koranic scriptures speak
about the earth being destroyed by fire, the sun and moon becoming darkened and the stars falling, believers being raised up to the
sky, the damned burning in Hell and Christ appearing on a cloud,
they are painting metaphorical images of the end times. These images represent internal truths about the fulfillment of the providence of restoration and should not be taken literally.

There are a number of important points to consider. First, the
earth that God made is devoid of evil. Nature has no intrinsic fall-
en characteristics. Why then would God want to destroy the earth
in the last days? How would doing so advance His providence of
restoration? And if believers could be physically raised from the
earth to the sky, why should they be? How would physical elevation change a person's relationship with God?

Why, too, would a loving God want to burn evildoers eternally in
fires of Hell? Would doing so please the loving Creator and spiritual
Parent of humankind? Would it fulfill His purpose in creating humanity and nature? And would it be just, considering that all people

are born into a fallen world without a choice in the matter and therefore cannot be held totally responsible for their wrong-doing? Then, too, is there any sin that deserves *eternal* punishment?

It is not the physical earth but evil that has to be destroyed, and evil can only be eliminated by the love and truth of God, never by literal fire. The 'earth' that has to be destroyed is a symbol of the world of Satan's dominion that has to be eradicated by the fire of God's love and truth. The false love of fallen relationships has to be replaced by the true love of God-centered relationships, resurrecting the spirits of fallen men and women from the depths of spiritual death in Hell to the heights of spiritual life in Heaven. It is the spirits of fallen individuals that will be raised up, not their bodies. Furthermore, those who have died physically exist only in the spirit world and are unable to live a physical life again, while those on earth can get no closer to God through the lifting up of their bodies.

There is no human sin that must be paid for with eternal damnation in Hell. If God had made human beings in such a way that they might be forever lost to their Creator, it would have been a failure by God. Religious history demonstrates God's absolute will to save every person who ever existed. If anyone is responsible for sin on earth it is Adam and Eve, since they gave Satan dominion over the first family, corrupting the very root of human lineage. And yet from the second generation of their family God sought to restore them. What's more, the whole thrust of history has been directed towards the restoration of Adam and Eve, as the Principle explanation of God's providence has shown. Since God has demonstrated His determination to save Adam and Eve, He must be equally determined to save everyone in their lineage, the rest of humankind, who bear less responsibility for the evil on earth.

The process of restoration is accomplished through the dispensation for true parents, who must bring to fallen humans both the truth and true love of God to defeat Satan's falsehoods and fallen love. The true father is the spiritual sun, the true mother the spiritual moon, and their children the spiritual stars. The light of the true family will overshadow the light of central figures who previously represented spiritual suns, moons and stars in the providence of restoration.

Unification of the World's Religions

Most founders and leaders of religions are now in the spirit world, many with centuries or millennia of spiritual work behind them. Their level of understanding is generally far higher than that of most people on earth, including those who follow, or try to follow, the spiritual paths that they pioneered. These high spirits can understand God's providence well, and they work to accomplish it from the spirit world. A core aspect of this understanding is the single purpose of God, under which all humanity is to be united as one, global family. Their cooperation with one another in the spirit world for the achievement of this goal produces a unifying tendency among the religious movements they founded.

No two people hold completely identical beliefs, but when all people use their own religious beliefs to reach maturity of spirit the divisions among people will be overcome by the power of true love. Thus the goal of unifying the world's religions is not to get everyone to adopt a single belief system, but for all believers to become true men and women who can build a world of peace and love, centered on God. It is to this end that religious leaders in the spirit world are working.

The Old History and The New

The last days simply means the last days of Satan's dominion on earth and the beginning of God's dominion. Thus the consummation of history is the turning point at which the old world of evil is superseded by the new world of good. History so far has been a history of the fallen world, but, beginning with the victory of true parents, it will become a history of good, as it would have been had the first humans not fallen.

There was a providence for the consummation of history at the time of Noah when through the flood God sought to end the world of evil and start a new world of good centered on Noah's family. Ham's failure resulted in a postponement of that providence. At the time of Jesus, God once more made all the preparations for the world of evil to be ended. Jesus and his bride were to fulfill the mission of true parents and establish the Kingdom of Heaven, but the crucifixion of Jesus resulted in another postponement of the providence. History since the time of Jesus has been directed towards preparing the whole world for true parents. With the success of their mission, the prophesies of the scriptures will be fulfilled and the consummation of fallen history will be accomplished.

Who are the True Parents?

The whole history of restoration has been directed towards laying a foundation for true parents, the payment of indemnity to enable God to send a man and woman to restore fallen Adam and Eve. Because of frequent delays in the fulfillment of these conditions, the only person God sent as a true parent after the fall was Jesus, and, because of John the Baptist's failure, Jesus himself was not able to fulfill the mission, having instead to offer his own life as a condition for the future fulfillment of God's will.

When an individual chosen for a particular mission in the history of restoration is unable to complete that mission another person is chosen in his place. For example, Abraham's mission was passed to Isaac and Isaac's to Jacob. Moses' mission was completed by Joshua, and the mission of building a temple was passed from King Saul to David and then Solomon. Elijah's return to prepare the way for Jesus was to be fulfilled by John the Baptist. Jesus came to complete the mission of Adam, but when the Israelites rejected him it became necessary for another person to inherit his mission, a true man to restore Adam and take a bride as restored Eve. Therefore, the true parents will be individuals given the mission of completing the restoration work of Jesus.

A providential person unable to complete his mission, for whatever reason, can indemnify that loss by supporting the person chosen to take his or her place. Thus Abraham indemnified the mistake in his sacrifice of animals by offering the life of his son as a condition to keep his family in the center of God's providence. In this way, Abraham participated in the victory of Isaac and was blessed accordingly. Jesus gave his life for the salvation of fallen humanity, but could not see the fulfillment of this mission in his lifetime. However, his offering of faith made a condition for the advent of the true parents, who will complete his mission.

True parents are unique figures in history not because of supernatural or superhuman attributes but because they accomplish God's will completely. They are a man and woman who have to earn the title of true parents through the payment of indemnity in perfect obedience to God. Given the strength of Satan and the extent of evil in the world, to accomplish that mission is possible only for individuals chosen specially for that purpose by God. True parents must have a remarkable standard of heart, with exceptional emotion, intellect and will, to understand God in sufficient depth to be able to carry out His mandate for restoration. They have to understand the root of evil and the way Satan has kept dominion over fallen humanity, and they have to gain complete victory over Satan, setting up a realm free from Satanic dominion where the three blessings can be fulfilled. To accomplish such a rigorous mission, they also need a strong constitution and good health.

When Will True Parents Come?

According to the Principle of Restoration, God can only send a central figure once a foundation of indemnity has been laid for that person. In the history of restoration it took 2000 years from the time of Abraham for the Children of Israel to lay a foundation for Jesus. Within that period, there were six major providential developments associated with laying that foundation. When Jesus was crucified, the work of restoring a world-wide foundation for true parents had to indemnify the mistakes of the previous two millennia. Hence the 2000 years after Jesus followed the pattern of 2000 years preparation for him.

These parallels in history indicate that the 20th Century is the time for true parents to come. More specifically, the 400 years of final preparation for true parents began in 1517 and was completed in 1917, at the end of World War I. However, the six time periods add up to a total of 1930 years, giving a spread of 13 years (1917–1930) for their advent.

The correct historical timing must coincide with circumstances suitable for the success of true parents' mission. There must be internal and external preparation of humankind for a sufficient number of enlightened people to respond wholeheartedly to God's new providence. As detailed in Chapter 20, these preparations were undertaken in the past four centuries when the whole world underwent a dramatic transformation.

Thus, by every providential measure, the time for true parents to come is *now*.

The Identity of the True Parents

Whoever fulfills the mission of restoring the fall of Adam and Eve, as well as all the many historic mistakes in the history of restoration, qualifies as true parents. There are many who claim messianic missions, based on inspirations they or others receive from the spirit world. What counts, though, is who fulfills the mission.

On August 24, 1992, before a large international audience of religious and political leaders, scientists, academics and journalists, gathered in Seoul, Korea, Sun Myung Moon announced that he and his wife Hak Ja Han had been chosen by God to be the true parents and had successfully accomplished their mission.

He was able to announce his mission forthrightly because of his accomplishments in life. He knew full well the skepticism with which his words would be received by many. He knew equally well, however, that those of good ancestral lineage and with integrity and goodness could easily recognize the verity of his claim. Good recognizes good, whereas those with questionable intentions are always suspicious of the intentions of others.

In this secular and scientific age, religion (and especially the new expression of religion) is viewed with distrust. Because of this, his efforts, as well as those of the millions of people associated with his Unification Movement, have frequently been the targets of bigoted attacks. It is a sign of the goodness of the movement and its founder that they have been so reviled by the world under Satan's dominion but also that they have consistently met these attacks with humility and love.

Born in Korea in 1920, at the age of sixteen Sun Myung Moon was commissioned by Jesus to complete his work. He spent all of his mature life in preparing for this mission and then carrying it out. After devoting nine years to discovering God's truth and finding out why the ideals of religion had not been fulfilled, he began teaching what he had learned, an outline of which has been presented in this book. Working diligently in Korea and Japan, and then America and the rest of the world, he built up a network of dedicated followers who have made his vision and teaching the basis for their lives of faith and the inspiration for a wide variety of projects designed to benefit humanity and help create a just world of true love. Always cooperating with believers from other faiths, members of the Unification Movement have launched many religious, cultural, educational, scientific and media activities aimed at creating inter-personal, inter-religious and international understanding and harmony.

Every step of the way has been wrought with difficulties and suffering. No established power, religious or secular, has fully embraced the Korean religious leader, and opposition to his teaching and activities has resulted in six spells in prison for him. For almost three years during the Korean war he was kept in a communist prison camp in North Korea, after being tortured to the edge of death. He also was imprisoned in South Korea, Japan and America, in every case because of his passionate teaching and ardent support for the causes in which he believes. Despite these trials and tribulations, he has never given up his mission. On the contrary, as with all true men and women of God, he has gained strength and broadened his following by overcoming all difficulties. In the process he has established an unrivaled foundation for human salvation and the creation of world peace.

In 1960 he was united with his bride in holy matrimony, fulfilling the second blessing. Since then, the True Parents have worked together as a couple to create a true family absolutely obedient to God, and have fulfilled all the conditions necessary to restore family, clan, tribe, nation and world. The love of their united heart is truly parental and global, embracing people of all races, nationalities and religions. On the foundation of their own blessing in 1960, they have offered the same marriage blessing to tens of thousands of couples, providing them with a foundation on which to build their own restored lineage.

The Completed Testament Age

On January 3, 1993, after all the necessary conditions had been fulfilled, Sun Myung Moon announced the beginning of the Completed Testament Age. This is the era for the realization of God's ideal on earth, centered on the foundation established by the True Parents. From this time God's power over human affairs increases dramatically, and the demarcation between good and evil, the fallen world and the true love world, becomes ever clearer. Although not yet evident to most people, for the first time in history good is in the ascendant position and evil declining. The signs of this positive change will proliferate rapidly as the providence of God advances with unprecedented and inexorable power.

Conclusion

Thus behind the chaos of the 20th Century world a spiritual revolution has quietly spread from Korea to all corners of the globe. It is not a political or military challenge to the status quo, but a transformation of hearts and minds that has affected the lives of millions, bringing changes to their families and the world. Through the victory of true parents, the marriage blessing is offered to couples from every race, religion and nation on earth, bringing them new meaning and a new standard of family life, and realizing a purification of lineage that offers future generations the real prospect of a completely different and good world. At the same time, these religious values for a unified world are being used to facilitate inter-religious understanding and harmony; cooperation among scientists; dialogues between political leaders; education in values for children and responsible media. This quiet revolution marks the consummation of the history of Satan's dominion over humanity and the beginning of God's Kingdom of Heaven on earth.

Readers are encouraged to determine for themselves whether this is true or not. God always responds to those who seek Him, and any sincere question will receive an answer. Through study and prayer, the veracity of the Principle and the identity of the True Parents can be confirmed.

GLOSSARY OF PRINCIPLE TERMS

Abel: The second son of Adam and the representative of God's side and original mind in humanity.

Angel: The highest creation prior to human beings. Angels are spirits without physical bodies, whose purpose is to serve men and women by helping them fulfill their purpose.

Blessing: The Unification Movement ceremony in which a man and woman are engrafted into the lineage of true parents as a married couple. It is a ceremony of rebirth and the starting point for that couple to establish a true family and to change their lineage from Satan's to God's dominion.

Blessings: God's endowment of human beings with His own attributes, in particular the three blessings. Human purpose is fulfilled through the completion of the three blessings.

Cain: The first son of Adam and the representative of Satan's side and fallen nature in humanity.

Cain and Abel Positions: As the sons of Adam and Eve, Cain and Abel were put in positions representing the two natures of their parents: fallen and original. The fallen nature came from the dominion of the Servant over Adam. Therefore, the relationship between Adam and the Servant has to be righted in the second generation of Adam's family. Cain represents the Servant and Abel represents Adam. When they restore the Adam-Servant relationship, they lay a foundation of substance for the restoration of Adam and Eve.

Central Figure: A person chosen to take Adam's position and restore the fall by making indemnity conditions to lay a foundation for true parents. Major central figures in the history of restoration were Noah, Abraham, Moses, Jesus, Mohammed, Buddha, Confucius, and so on. Also, each individual is the central figure of his or her own restoration, and must make a personal foundation to restore their fallen nature and receive true parents.

Change of Lineage: The process whereby fallen men and women leave the realm of Satan's dominion in the sinful lineage of Adam and Eve and are reborn into the realm of God's dominion in the sinless lineage of true parents through an engrafting process. (The blessing is the ceremony associated with this process.)

Commandment: The instruction to Adam and Eve from God prohibiting them from "eating the forbidden fruit", which meant they were not permitted to engage in illicit love.

Conscience: The interaction of the spirit mind and physical mind centered on truth during the formation of the original mind. It is the moral voice of human mind and the object of original mind. It directs humans to the fulfillment of their true purpose as beings of absolute value.

Consummation of History: The time period when Satan's sovereignty of evil is ended and God's sovereignty of good begins.

Death: There are two kinds of human death: the natural death of the physical body and the spiritual death of separation from God, the source of life. Physical death is a natural and good phenomenon occurring in accordance with the principles of creation. Through the human fall, Adam and Eve died spiritually, establishing a lineage of spiritually dead descendants.

Direct Dominion: After passing through the three stages of growth by obeying God's laws, human beings enter into the direct dominion of God's love, a state of oneness with God's heart. In this state, any act that would separate them from God would be unthinkable. With perfectly mature love there is nothing to limit humans because anything they do is in oneness with God and produces goodness.

Divine Spirits: The spirits of human beings who have achieved oneness with God after completing the growing process through fulfilling the three blessings. They are true men and women.

Dual Characteristics: Elements common to all creation, which derive from the dual attributes of the Creator, God. The primary dual characteristics of internal character and external form shape the identity of beings; the secondary dual characteristics of positivity and negativity differentiate creations into complementary pairs which interact in the dynamics of life: existence, action and multiplication.

Engrafting: The process whereby fallen men and women are reborn into the lineage of true parents. This is accomplished through the blessing ceremony.

Evil (and Good): Anything that contributes to the fulfillment of God's ideal, meaning the three blessing, is good. Consequently, everything that blocks the way toward this fulfillment is evil. Thoughts and actions that create a base for God are good, while those which create a base for Satan are evil. In other words, when a subject and object give and receive centered on God's purpose for the creation, good is produced, but when a subject and object interact in violation of God's purpose they create evil. Things are neither good nor evil in themselves; the purpose they are used for determines their value.

Evil Spirits: The spirits of human beings who live in violation of God's principles and therefore are most remote from Him. These spirits manifest ugliness and evil and are the enemies of God and goodness. They influence other human beings to disobey God as well.

External Form: The visible expression of identity in a tangible structure and form, it is the embodiment of a being's internal character. God's external form is Universal Prime Energy. In nature it is manifested as human, animal or plant bodies and molecular or atomic structures.

Fallen Nature: In the process of the fall the original good nature of Adam and Eve got twisted into fallen nature with four particular aspects: failing to take God's viewpoint, standing out of the given position, reversing dominion and multiplying evil. This fallen nature was passed from Adam and Eve to all of their descendants, preventing them from becoming one with God.

First Blessing: The human ability and right to become an individual with perfect personality and to achieve the value of a complete, true being, sharing God's value. Those who achieve mind-body unity centered on God become one with God's will, have godly personalities and become objects of joy for God. As true men and women, they fulfill the first blessing and are thereby qualified to fulfill the second and third blessings.

Forces of Giving and Receiving Action: The forces generated by giving and receiving between subject and object. These forces are the substantial foundation for life itself: existence, action and multiplication.

Form Spirits: The spirits of human beings who have achieved an initial, formation stage level of spiritual growth. They are not purposefully evil, but neither are they focused on obeying and serving God. Their's is a servant's attitude, motivated by fear more than love.

Formation Stage Spirit World: The spiritual realm of initial growth towards oneness with God and the level achieved by form spirits.

Foundation of Faith: The condition of indemnity to restore the failure of Adam and Eve to believe God's commandment. A foundation of faith is laid by someone who takes Adam's position and demonstrates faith in the word of God by making a significant offering and keeping an attitude of obedience for a meaningful period of time. A foundation of faith is the necessary starting point for a foundation of substance and foundation for true parents.

Foundation of Substance: The condition of indemnity to restore the fallen nature of Adam and Eve. The foundation of substance is laid by representatives of Adam and the Servant restoring the relationship that was destroyed when the Servant unrighteously dominated Adam through the fall, planting in him the fallen nature that has bedeviled humankind.

Foundation for True Parents: The condition of indemnity necessary for true parents to appear in history. The Foundation for True Parents is made up of the combined foundations of faith and substance.

Four Position Foundation: Through giving and receiving, a subject and object create a new entity which embodies elements of both. This new creation adds a fourth position to the three occupied by God, subject and object. This is the foundation for the fulfillment of the purpose of creation. All beings are completed through perfecting relationships within the four position foundation.

Free Will: The human capacity to choose, with which God endowed men and women. If exercised in accordance with God's will, it enables humans to perfect love. If exercised in disobedience to God's will, it results in separation from God. There is no true freedom without responsibility and no responsibility without freedom.

Fruit: The fruit of a particular tree in the Garden of Eden was the one thing forbidden to Adam and Eve. It was a symbol of Eve's love. Eating the fruit before being permitted to do so by God meant indulging in premature sexual relations.

Giving and Receiving Action: The relationship of giving and receiving energy between a subject and object which draws them together until each finds completion through its relationship with the other, creating unity. This action generates forces of giving and receiving action.

God: The good and loving Creator of the universe and all the principles which govern it. As the invisible Parent of humankind, God is the origin of human love, life and lineage.

Good (and Evil): Anything that contributes to the fulfillment of God's ideal, meaning the three blessing, is good. Consequently, everything that blocks the way toward this fulfillment is evil. Thoughts and actions that create a base for God are good, while those which create a base for Satan are evil. In other words, when a subject and object give and receive centered on God's purpose for the creation, goodness is produced, but when a subject and object interact in violation of God's purpose they create evil. Things are neither good nor evil in themselves; the purpose they are used for determines their value.

Heart: The irrepressible impulse to experience joy through love. The internal character of God, Heart is the foundation of His being and oneness, the source of His love and the origin of His purpose in making the creation. In creation, heart is the core of human internal character and human mind, and the source of human purpose and love. The fundamental essence of heart is the parental desire to create and love offspring.

Heaven: The realm of God's direct dominion of love, in which human beings who have completed the purpose of creation exist eternally, as divine spirits, in oneness with God. Heaven is a location only in the sense that it exists wherever God's love is expressed fully by true men and women. Because the body is needed for spiritual growth, Heaven must be created on earth by human beings fulfilling their purpose, before it can exist in the spiritual world.

Hell: The realm of spirit world inhabited by evil spirits: those human beings most distant from God. Hell is the realm of falsehood and disobedience to God, where love is impure and human relationships mock God's ideal of creation. People at this low level of existence are in Hell while living on earth and after their bodies die. Hell is a location only in the sense that it exists wherever human beings give and receive in disobedience to the will of God. Hell was created on earth first, through the human fall.

History of Restoration: The sequence of events related to God's work to restore fallen humanity to a relationship of oneness with God. This history encompasses all the main figures of Biblical and Koranic history, as well as the other significant religious figures of the world. The object of restoration history is the restoration of Adam and Eve in the personages of the true parents.

Human Fall: The separation of Adam and Eve from God through their disobedient and unprincipled acts of love, committed under the influence of the Servant.

Human Mind: The invisible, spiritual aspect of a human being which provides direction and purpose to human existence. In a person who is physically alive, the spirit mind interacts with the physical mind in creating the human mind. After the physical body dies, the physical mind ceases to exist but the human mind exists forever.

Iblis: The Koranic jinn (or angel) assigned by God to care for Adam and Eve, who seduced Eve and became Satan. He is called the Servant in this text.

Indemnity: In order for humans to restore their original state they must fulfill their responsibility by making certain conditions which indemnify the loss caused by disobedience. These are called indemnity conditions. Payment of indemnity qualifies people to become free from Satan's dominion and united with God.

Indirect Dominion: the stage of human growth in which God relates to human beings through the mediation of His laws. At this stage individuals are not completely accessible and responsive to God, but by obeying God's instructions they can learn how to perfect their love and enter the direct dominion of God. During this period people must exercise complete responsibility under the conditions of their God-given freedom.

Individual Truth Body: Whenever a creation becomes a unified being of harmonized dual characteristics, and completes a four position foundation it reflects the unity of God, and embodies His Truth. It is then called an individual truth body.

Internal Character: The invisible aspect of being that determines its uniqueness, purpose and direction. The internal character of God is Heart, the origin of emotion, intellect and will. In creation it is manifested as human mind, instinctive animal or plant mind and the internal directive aspect of physico-chemical reality.

Life Element: The truth and love that originate in God and flow from Him to humans, providing them with the spiritual elements they need to grow to perfection.

Life Spirits: The spirits of human beings who have achieved the growth stage level of spiritual growth. They are like adopted sons of God, learning to love instead of fear Him, but not yet having fulfilled their purpose and reached full maturity as true men and women.

Lineage: The transmittance of characteristics and conditions from generation to generation. In the creation process, human beings were endowed with God's attributes. They were to inherit His nature and His standard of unconditional love and thus become part of His lineage. Through the fall, however, they failed to embody God's attributes or emulate His love. Thus human lineage transmitted fallen nature and imperfect, fallen love from generation to generation.

Lucifer: The Biblical archangel assigned by God to care for Adam and Eve, who seduced Eve and became Satan. He is called the Servant in this text.

Messiah: The messiah is a new Adam who must perfect himself and his bride. Together they become true parents. He is chosen by God to save fallen humanity by fulfilling the three blessings and thus providing the way for fallen men and women to be separated from Satan and united with God by engrafting onto the sinless lineage of true parents. Jesus came as the messiah but was murdered before he could take a bride and complete the mission.

Object: The responding partner in the relationship of giving and receiving with a subject, within and among created beings. Subject and object are not value-differentiated but complementary characteristics essential for life.

Obsession: When one spirit unrighteously dominates the spirit of another person. Since only low spirits would seek to dominate other people for their own, selfish benefit, obsessive relationships are always negative in result. Many mental illnesses can be attributed to spirit obsessions.

Offering: A condition of indemnity paid by a central figure to lay a foundation of faith. This could be prayer, fasting, tithing, or any form of pure giving to God and other human beings.

Original Mind: The perfect relationship between the spirit mind and physical mind, in which the spirit mind maintains its subject role over the physical mind, centered on God. The original mind is perfected human mind.

Paradise: The realm of spirit world entered into at the growth stage of human maturation. It is inhabited by life spirits.

Parallels in History: The re-occurrence of similar events on parallel time lines in the history of restoration, caused by patterns in the human response to God, in particular the patterns of success and failure in laying foundations for true parents.

Perfection: It is achieved when a created being completely fulfills the purpose for which it was created. A human being becomes perfect when he/she reaches full maturity of character, when actions of the body are in absolute harmony with the God-centered mind and when the individual is in complete unity of love with God.

Physical Body: The external part of the physical person which communicates with the surrounding physical world through five physical senses. Its shape and functions correspond to the internal, spiritual nature of the human being and it is the organism through which human beings can multiply.

Physical Fall: The premature love relationship between Adam and Eve.

Physical Mind: The causal part of the physical person which is similar to an animal's instinct and manifests desires for nourishment, self-protection, comfort and reproduction.

Physical Person: The temporary part of a human being which begins its existence at conception, grows to maturity and dies. It lives in the physical world within the limits of time and space. It is a necessary part of the human opportunity to perfect love and to multiply descendants.

Physical Senses: Sight, taste, touch, hearing and smell, which are attributes of the physical body that enable it to interact with the physical world.

Physical World: The universe limited by time and space which can be experienced through the five physical senses. It is the realm of existence characterized by the cycle of birth, physical growth and death. It is also the temporary environment where human beings perfect their ability to give and receive love as well as multiply the human species.

Positivity and Negativity: Dual characteristics that enable every being to interact with others to create a harmonious union from which the creation is formed and multiplied. These are not value-differentiated but complementary characteristics essential for life. God's positivity and negativity are original masculinity and femininity. In creation, positivity and negativity are manifested as human, animal or plant masculinity and femininity, and as molecular, atomic and sub-atomic positive and negative charges.

Predestination: God's plan for human beings, which is fulfilled when they complete their portion of responsibility in obedience to God.

Principles of Creation: The principles according to which God made and governs His creation. They derive from the principles of His own perfect being and are manifested in the spiritual laws of faith and the physical laws of the universe. Through these the all-important purpose for creation is known.

Principles of Restoration: These are the principles of creation applied to the restoration process of fallen humankind. They can be summarized as follows: human restoration is re-creation which is accomplished through the payment of indemnity.

Possession: When a spirit takes control of another person's physical body and uses that person for his or her own purposes. This produces the phenomenon of a split personality, or schizophrenia, since there are two spirits vying for control of a single body. If more than one foreign spirit occupies a body, the result is witnessed as a multiple personality disorder. Since only low spirits would seek to dominate another person's body for their own, selfish benefit, possessive relationships are always negative in result. As indicated, many mental illnesses can be attributed to spirit possessions.

Rebirth: The change of lineage from the fallen realm of Satan's dominion to the restored realm of God's dominion. This is accomplished by engrafting into true parents' lineage.

Reincarnation: The mistaken view that human spirits dwell in more than one body in order to work out their karma, which is their responsibility to others. The phenomena that contribute to the formation of this notion are actually phenomena of returning resurrection.

Responsibility: The effort human beings must make to obey God's will. Through fulfillment of their responsibility, men and women grow to completion. There is no true freedom without responsibility and no responsibility without freedom.

Restoration: Salvation through the return of fallen, sinful humanity to a state of purity and oneness with God. It takes place through three stages of spiritual growth by payment of indemnity in reversing the disobedience of Adam, Eve and the Servant, and, ultimately, engrafting into the sinless lineage of true parents.

Resurrection: The process of restoring spiritual life to the spiritually dead.

Returning Resurrection: The return of spirits to the physical world to participate in resurrection, which is always led by central figures working a new providence among people on earth. By serving individuals involved in a resurrection providence on earth, spirit men and women can benefit from the vitality elements of those working on earth and themselves be resurrected.

Sacrifice: The offering of one's possessions or oneself to God to lay a foundation of faith. Also the offering of one's possessions and oneself in service to others to lay a foundation of substance.

Salvation: Restoration of fallen humans to a state of oneness with God. This is achieved through individuals fulfilling their responsibilities, in obedience to God. Ultimately, salvation is accomplished when fallen men and women leave the lineage of Satan and enter the lineage of God through grafting onto the sinless lineage of true parents.

Satan: The identity of the Servant after he fell. Having disobeyed God, the Servant became the great enemy of God and worked to prevent human beings from fulfilling the three blessings. Satan is an invisible spiritual being who influences people through their spirits. In a wider meaning, Satan is any spiritual influence that is in harmony with Satan and opposed to God.

Second Blessing: The human ability and right to create an ideal family and world through fulfilling true love relationships, sharing God's ability to create life and raise children. When a man and a woman create a true love family, they fulfill the second blessing. That family gives joy to God.

Serpent: The symbolic creature that tempted Adam and Eve to fall. The Serpent was in fact the Servant, known as Lucifer in the Bible and Iblis in the Koran. He became known as Satan after the fall.

Servant, The: A spiritual being described in Holy Scriptures as playing the key role in leading the first man and woman into their fall from God. In the Bible, the Servant is an archangel Lucifer; in the Koran he is the Jinn or angel Iblis.

Sin: An act or thought which violates God's principles and creates a base for giving and receiving with Satan, directly or indirectly. Sin separates human beings from God and from one another.

Spirit Body: The external part of the spirit person which communicates with the surrounding spiritual world through five spiritual senses. It has a definite shape corresponding to the individual characteristics of the spirit mind.

Spirit Elements: The energy generated for the physical person (body) by the spirit person (spirit). Interaction with God's love and truth and good spirits generates good spirit elements which inspire the body to do good. Interaction with falsehood, hatred and evil spirits generates evil spirit elements which motivate the body to do evil.

Spirit Mind: The causal part of the spirit person and the seat of the human desire for joy, love and beauty. It is the source of emotion, intellect and will, and the part of human beings which can resonate perfectly with God.

Spirit Person: The causal part of a human being which begins its autonomous existence at the birth of a baby. It is not limited by time and space and after the death of the physical person it exists eternally in the spirit world.

Spirit World: The unlimited, invisible and causal universe that is known to the five spiritual senses. It is the substantial, eternal home of human spirits.

Spiritual Fall: The illicit love relationship between the Servant and Eve.

Spiritual Senses: Counterparts to the five physical senses that are attributes of the spiritual body and enable it to interact with the spiritual world.

Stages of Growth: There are three fundamental stages in the growing period through which every created being passes: formation, growth and completion. A being can fulfill its proper place in the order of the universe only by completing these three stages of growth.

Subject: The initiator of the relationship of giving and receiving with an object, within and among created beings. Subject and object are not value-differentiated but complementary characteristics essential for life.

Third Blessing: The human ability and right to have dominion over the rest of creation, sharing God's capacity to make and modify things. When families tend to nature with true love and create a harmonious relationship between humankind and the rest of creation, they fulfill the third blessing. Such a world gives joy to God.

Three Blessings: The blessings with which God endowed the first human ancestors, Adam and Eve, after they were created. They encompass the purpose of human life and the aspirations for all human beings. *(See separately first, second and third blessing.)*

Trinity: The ideal relationship between God, a true man and a true woman, which is the foundation for the creation of a true family and lineage. The original trinity was God, Adam and Eve, but it was invaded by Satan. Jesus, who came to restore Adam, could not take a bride during his life on earth, so after he ascended to the spirit world the Holy Spirit worked with him in the position of a spiritual bride, in the place of Eve. Ultimately, the Adam and Eve positions of the original trinity are fulfilled by true parents.

Triple Object Purpose: The four position foundation is a perfect unit of human relationships because it provides each of its members with three different types of objects with whom it can perfect the full range of giving and receiving relationships of love. Each individual creation is completed through its primary relations with three objects within the four position foundation. Thus the triple object purpose is the key to fulfillment of the purpose of creation.

True Family: The basic unit of human society created by a true man and a true woman united in love as parents of true children. This is the environment where children can grow to become true parents themselves, where true men and women are multiplied in God's creation. True families naturally expand into tribes and nations to create a true world. The true family is the model of ideal life and relationships and the standard for human values.

True Love: The fundamental impulse of God's Heart. This is the impulse of parental heart to give unconditionally to His creation and the source of life for humanity and creation. The nature of true love is to give without calculation or reservation. A true man and a true woman have the characteristics to be fully endowed with God's true love and together form the nucleus of a true love family, society, nation and world.

True Man and True Woman: A man and woman who have united mind and body into perfect oneness centered on God's ideal. A true man is the image of God's masculinity; a true woman the image of God's femininity.

True Parents: A true man and true woman united in love centered on God's ideal who are qualified to give birth to true children. True parents together are the complete embodiment of the dual attributes of God and the completed image of God. They inherit and pass on to their lineage true parenthood and true love. Historically, the first man and woman to complete the ideal of God's creation qualify as the True Parents of humankind. They establish a new, pure lineage of God and give rebirth to fallen humanity by engrafting them into their own family. This new lineage eventually supplants the lineage dominated by Satan and is the starting point for the creation of a God-centered world.

Unification Movement: The activities, projects and organizations inspired by the vision of Sun Myung Moon (and in many cases founded by him) and guided by the ideals and understanding of the Unification Principle. It is not a legal entity.

Unification Principle: The essential teachings of Sun Myung Moon, it is an explanation of human beings and nature based on belief in the existence of God, the good and loving Creator of all beings and the origin of the principles that govern human life. It explains the relationship between Creator and creation and demonstrates God's existence as revealed in His creation and in the history of humankind. Also called the Principle, it provides the basis for the unification of the human family centered on God.

Unification of Religions: The harmonization of various faiths under the parental love of God.

Universal Prime Energy: God's external form, it is the expression of God's love and the intangible source of life out of which the creation was made.

Universal Prime Force: Universal Prime Energy in action. God endows His creation with universal prime force, which is the directed energy that sustains creation's existence, action and multiplication.

Vitality Elements: The energy generated through the activities of the physical person (body) for the growth of the spirit person (spirit). Good deeds generate good vitality elements which support the healthy development of the spirit. Evil deeds generate evil vitality elements which deform the spirit.